W9-CVN-880

Brother Kawabe

by
Glen Williamson

Light and Life Press
Winona Lake, Indiana 46590

Copyright © 1977 by
Light and Life Press

All rights reserved. No part of this book may be reproduced in any form,
except for brief quotations in reviews, without the written permission of the
publisher.

ISBN 0-89367-012-X

Printed in the United States of America by
Light and Life Press
Winona Lake, Indiana
46590

DEDICATION

To Bishop Takesaburo Uzaki, who contends
for the faith once delivered
unto the saints and which so beautifully
characterized Brother Kawabe.

CONTENTS

INTRODUCTION
by
Bishop Elmer E. Parsons

Teikichi Kawabe was a great Christian. He lived a long, fruitful, and steadfast life. Born in feudal Japan, his life covered an era of upheaval and radical change. Like a series of earthquakes, his country suffered the shocks of moving from a medieval society into the modern world. The Industrial Revolution, a late desperate grasp at colonial acquisition and expansion, the religious fanaticism associated with worship of the Emperor, militarism, and finally the defeat in World War II shook the body and soul of Japan.

To be a Christian during this period was often unpopular and dangerous. Almost without exception, becoming a Christian created rifts within one's family. Yet, through all these turbulent years, Brother Kawabe set the course of his life in an unswerving path. He was like a patriarch and prophet combined. Above all he was a faithful disciple of Jesus Christ.

Dr. Glen Williamson, in this book, has captured the spirit of Brother Kawabe. Much more could and should be said about this great man. But enough is presented here to let us know that a mighty Christian has lived among us.

Brother Kawabe's life influenced thousands of people outside the circle of his immediate church. While he was for all practical purposes the founder of the Free Methodist Church in Japan, his name was known in greater circles than the name of the church itself. It was my privilege to know Brother Kawabe during his final years. I was blessed by this association. He radiated the strength and serenity of a saint. People solicited his prayers. He had a delightful ability to see the absurd and the humorous in a given situation.

As recounted in the book, the last years of his life were spent in blindness. I recall taking him one of his first tastes of ice cream after World War II. Since he could not see the ice cream he sensed a pleasant delight when it touched his lips. "My stomach is sure going to be surprised," was his whimsical comment.

I attended the funeral of Reverend Kawabe. It was my privilege to present a eulogy. It was not a sad event, but a coronation, a celebration of a life well lived.

I commend this book to its readers. May your life be touched by the life story of this good man, and may you share in his firm commitment to Jesus Christ as Lord and Saviour.

1

Yosuke Matsuoka

Osaka, a bustling metropolis south and west of Tokyo, was numbered among the larger cities of the globe when World War II got underway. Its teeming millions of hard-working people, however, could hardly comprehend what was taking place in the world or just where their native Japan fit into the complicated puzzle, which was already spattered with blood.

Now they were told that Yosuke Matsuoka, Japan's minister of foreign affairs, had visited Europe at the invitation of Adolph Hitler. There, it was reported, he met the fuhrer and Mussolini and signed with them the Tripartite Pact forming an alliance between their nations, which historians ever after would refer to as the Axis Powers. Just what this meant was not clear to the man on the street, but he knew that something would have to give way soon.

The people, however, were about to be enlightened, so the newspapers, posters, and blaring radio bulletins proclaimed. Matsuoka, himself, was holding a mass meeting in Osaka to explain firsthand just where Japan stood among the other world powers, each of which was squaring off to enter history's greatest holocaust. Thousands of people poured into the auditorium as the regal statesman with round face, close-cropped hair, black mustache, and large horn-rimmed glasses took his place on the platform.

In the audience one might have seen an elderly gentleman take a pen and pad from his pocket and scribble a hurried note. The man's soft, benign countenance emerged in startling contrast to the taut, bleak faces around him, yet no one would have said he appeared passive and unconcerned. He bore every mark of a humble clergyman whose dedicated life, clean heart, and brilliant mind were prepared to render him relaxed and calm in any time of trouble. His shyness and humility were showing through so plainly, however, that a stranger would hardly have given him a second look.

Perhaps that is why an astonished usher stared with amazement as the calm little man instructed him to take the note to Mr. Matsuoka and *wait for a reply*.

"Go!" the man said with a firmness that belied his humble manner. "Go, before it is too late!"

The youth accepted the note with hesitation.

"Go!" the old one commanded again, and the usher hurried away.

With fear and embarrassment he mounted the platform and cautiously approached the mighty leader, wondering what would be his fate if the missive were a threat or worse from a madman.

But there was no problem. The statesman read the note, smiled, and scribbled his reply.

"Be sure my friend gets this at once," he said. The usher, greatly relieved, hurried back to the calm little man.

Matsuoka's speech was an oratorical triumph in which he extolled the grievances of the nation, explained the necessity of conquest, and then closed with an emotional plea for the unwavering allegiance of every citizen throughout the awful days which surely were ahead.

When the meeting was over, the little missionary, whose name was Teikichi Kawabe, made his way to the hotel where Matsuoka was staying. He waited in the lobby until exactly midnight, showed the note to the clerk, and was ushered at once to the dignitary's elaborate suite, according to the written instructions.

The meeting of the two friends was a happy one. "My days are so full," the great one explained, "I knew I could not get to Awaji Island to see you. I am so glad you came here tonight. I need your counsel and your prayers."

"I can only pray that God's will be done," the missionary responded softly.

"Yes, I know," agreed the statesman. "What we are about to do you cannot possibly understand. Only believe me that we are doing the best we know for our land and our people."

The strange friendship between the two men had begun many years before in America where Matsuoka received his education. He was graduated at an early age from the University of Oregon School of Law. As a boy in Japan, he was unusually brilliant, aggressive, and so headstrong that by the time he reached the age of thirteen, the generation gap was great. To ease the strain at home, his parents arranged for the boy to accompany an uncle to the United States. By the time the ship dropped anchor in America, however, the distracted relative, unable to manage the mischievous, self-centered youngster, turned him ashore to find for himself how cruel the world can be to one who thinks he knows all the answers.

The lad, weary and footsore, drifted into a Methodist mission, where he was befriended by Mr. Kawabe, a man seventeen years his senior, who eventually led him to Christ. Hence a profound friendship was established that was to endure many tests of time and circumstances.

Later Mr. Kawabe accepted an offer by the Free Methodist Church to evangelize and open churches in his native Japan. Before leaving America, he helped work out a plan for Yosuke Matsuoka to make his home with an American family in Portland, Oregon. It proved to be a congenial arrangement.

Much later, when Matsuoka returned to Japan, he made his way at once to Awaji Island to visit his old friend Kawabe. It was then he told of his desire to enter the diplomatic service of Japan. With proper respect for age and experience, he asked the missionary to advise him and to remember him in prayer.

"If that is your calling," the good man answered, "I know of no reason why you should not pursue it. But you must receive a Japanese education. Your American training will be most helpful as a diplomat, but it alone is not sufficient to prepare you for service to our country."

Matsuoka saw the wisdom of this advice and enrolled in a Japanese school. He soon won his way into the diplomatic corps. His rise to fame and fortune was swift. In addition to the governmental posts he held, he eventually became president of the South Manchurian Railroad, and in 1940 he was named Minister of Foreign Affairs in Prince Konoye's cabinet. Later he was relieved of this position, but there is little doubt that he was involved in the planning of the infamous attack on Pearl Harbor.

It is difficult, of course, to conceive of his being a practicing Christian through his years in national leadership. Late in life, he made the following statement: "While I am a Christian, I am a Matsuoka Christian. I don't believe a lot of things that they have attached to the regular sects in America and Europe."

These words are altogether too revealing. But there is no disputing the fact that, while he apparently discounted much of his earlier training, his faith in the integrity and prayers of the one who led him to the Lord more than forty years before never wavered even to the day of his death. He continued his hurried visits to Awaji Island for prayer and counsel in the busiest days of his political career.

The news media made much of those visits and published in glaring headlines that the foreign minister again had come to the island to see his oldest friend, the Reverend Teikichi Kawabe.[1]

Finally in the echo of atomic blasts the war came to a grinding halt. General MacArthur took supreme command of the government, and Emperor Hirohito shook the people with the startling denouncement of his divinity. It was impossible for Americans, who were resting in the security of a victorious homeland, to understand the frustration and darkness that settled like a shroud over the war-torn islands of Japan.

Teikichi Kawabe spent long hours in prayer entreating the God of heaven to bring order out of chaos, to bring glory to His name, and above all to bring revival to Japan. Then came an announcement that was almost more than the tenderhearted minister could bear. Tojo, along with seven other war criminals, was under indictment, and it was a foregone conclusion that they would face death at the close of their trials. Among the names released was Yosuke Matsuoka!

Again the little missionary groaned at the feet of his Master: "Do not allow my friend — mistaken as he must have been — to suffer the horror and disgrace of death upon the gallows. Deliver him!" he cried in anguish, until his own strength was almost gone.

God still works in mysterious ways.... During the trial, June 27, 1946, Yosuke Matsuoka died of natural causes in his cell at the age of sixty-six. Seven years later, Mr. Kawabe slipped away to heaven.

The remaining chapters of this book give a running account of the nearly unbelievable fruit-bearing life of Teikichi Kawabe, a man called of God for a particular hour. For more than sixty years, in missionary circles of his church around the world, he was known as *Brother Kawabe.*

---

[1]While in Japan, doing research for this work, it was my privilege to have Dr. Kazuhito Shimada, pastor of the Fukura Free Methodist Church on Awaji Island, translate a number of those newspaper accounts. — GW

2

Restless Ambition

Following the earthshaking discovery in 1492 of an unknown hemisphere that embraced two great continents and reached nearly from pole to pole, all Europe began to buzz with plans for conquest. It was understood soon that the New World separated Europe from what must have seemed to be the backside of the Far East. The ancient fear of unchartered seas ending in bottomless cataracts or worse was forever abolished. Asia and the Americas became targets to conquer.

Tiny vessels, depending solely on wind, muscle, and good fortune to keep them on their ways, rode the swells of the Atlantic and Pacific waters for centuries before the first steamship made its appearance. Adventure, gold, and power were the principal motivations of the reckless seamen who defied the elements in their passion for conquest. Now and then, though, dedicated missionaries were discovered riding along, determined also to conquer, to "Go . . . into all the world and preach the gospel to every creature."

The first missionary to set foot on Japanese soil was a devout Roman Catholic, Francis Xavier, who arrived in 1549 with a band of Portuguese sailors.

Protestants, of course, wish it might have been a son of the Reformation who first spoke the name of Christ to the idol worshipers of Japan. But the Lord, who sees the end from the beginning, must have had His hand upon the situation all the way. In any event, Father Xavier was a determined moralist who cried out against the prevailing sins of idolatry, sodomy, and abortion in terms so strong that his interpreters often found it hard to convey the message with equivalent force.

But his message made sense, and weary listeners, tired of sin and corruption, fell humbly, gratefully at his feet. Many of his converts began to preach the message too, and after forty years there were those who still crusaded in the same vein. By then, in an annual report received by the general of the Jesuit order in Rome, a total of 200 churches, twenty hospitals, and 150 thousand converts was enumerated.

Father Xavier's ministry, of course, left much to be desired from a strictly evangelical point of view, but his Japanese converts were unaware of this. The redeeming factor (from that same viewpoint) lies in the fact that the association of the Christian religion with clean moral living was firmly established. Later, Catholic teachers dropped this emphasis.

The idea, however, was deeply implanted, and generations later, when Protestant missionaries came demanding a high moral standard of conduct for their converts, Japanese Christians tended to view the movement as a revival of the old, rather than as an innovation of something new.

Probably this concept was an important factor in Protestantism's phenomenal growth in the years that followed. By 1972 there were twice as many Protestants as Catholics in Japan.[1]

In 1582, a little more than three decades after Japan's introduction to Christianity, a brilliant, ruthless dictator named Hideyoshi came into power. It was not long before he became suspicious of the "foreign religion" and began to expel priests and destroy churches. He ushered in an almost unbelievable era of persecution. Hundreds of

[1]For a detailed study of this, see "Understanding Japan" by Dr. Lavern Snider at the close of this book (Appendix A). For further background on the religious life of Japan, read "Religions of Japan" written in 1950 by Miss Ruth Mylander, now deceased, who spent many years in Japan under the Free Methodist Missionary Board (Appendix B).

Catholic Christians were put to death, and thousands more were exiled.

Hideyoshi was succeeded, following his death, by a professing Buddhist named Ieyasu. In turn, he conferred his office and power to a son, Hidetada, who saw — and probably promoted — a veritable reign of terror. Despicable tortures were introduced. For instance, men were sawed in pieces, and others were forced to stand beneath a deluge of near-boiling water that gushed from hot springs out of the bowels of the earth. It was believed that more than 275 thousand Christians were persecuted without mercy between 1614 and 1635.

By then, Japan had entered a period of isolationism which was to last for 250 years. During that time, no one was allowed to leave the island; and except for a few friendly, peaceful Dutchmen, no outsider was allowed to land upon its shores. Martyrdom became common, while nominal Christians recanted by the thousands until it was believed that the "foreign religion" was stamped out completely. But Christianity hides best, not in caves and catacombs, but in the hearts of believers. The churches were closed, but the God of Abraham, Isaac, and Jacob never left the islands of Japan.

The great, overwhelming number of people, however, who had never come into close contact with the church considered the Christian religion an enemy of the people, and they hated it with a vengeance. What they didn't understand was why its adherents were willing to undergo the suffering and death that had been imposed upon them. And this knowledge probably disturbed their peace of mind far more than they were willing to admit.

Thousands of families fell into this category, and by the middle of the nineteenth century one such clan resided in Fukuoka Prefecture. This was an enterprising Buddhist family, the head of which was well known in his hometown of Yamada as Seizaburo Kawabe. The

Kawabes' second son, Teikichi, was born in 1864. He is the *Brother Kawabe* of our story.

Teikichi's birth followed by just eleven years a critical event in Japanese history that was to change the whole life-style of the nation. Japan's isolationism came to an end when a mighty battleship, proudly bearing the stars and stripes, came to rest in Tokyo Bay. It was an electrifying experience for the people of the island who expected the mammoth cannons to belch balls of fire and lead upon their cities. The armed vessel, however, was manned by a friendly admiral named Commodore Perry, who was determined to open the doors of Japan to a new epic of international fellowship, peace, and prosperity. And he did exactly that.

From that tense hour, Japan underwent an unprecedented process of change, an unbelievable era of progress in every area of its existence. And Teikichi Kawabe grew up with it.

By the time Teikichi reached adolescence, his father sensed in him a certain restless ambition and marked aptitude for making money. And if it were not for the fact that he had been endowed with a remarkable bent for honesty, his youthful friends would have no doubt suffered severe losses in their little dealings with him.

By 1880, when Teikichi reached the adventurous age of seventeen, the restless ambition that constantly dogged his steps succeeded in leading him away from his home, his father, and his older brothers and others to seek fame and fortune. Unlike the ambitious prodigal son in Jesus' story, however, Teikichi had no intentions of wasting his substance in riotous living. He was determined to find the good life in the accumulation of wealth and the security it would provide.

The elder Kawabe knew there was little hope of deterring his son who had laid his plans well. So he sent him forth with his blessing, admonishing him to remain true always to his Buddhist faith. He was sure the granting of good fortune was the sole prerogative of the gods. At the same time he warned him to shun at all costs the Christian teachings which, with the opening of the nation's doors, were experiencing revival. Teikichi promised to follow his father's advice, for, intellectually, he was in accord with it. Spiritually, though, he had never sensed any degree of peace or benefit from his allegiance to Buddha.

He went first to the bustling metropolis of Osaka to spread his wings. He reasoned well that to deal in the everyday necessities of life was the surest and speediest road to success. Hence, his first job of selling rice and candles was a lucrative venture. This humble sales position, however, was just a stepping-stone to the fulfillment of a magnificent dream — that of building a commercial empire of his own. And since that air castle was international in scope, he spent his spare hours studying the English language. He faced a problem in that he had no close associate with whom to communicate in the strange tongue; hence, he found his progress to be slow. It was too slow for the ambitious Teikichi, so he went to Tokyo in search of another position and a better opportunity to find practical assistance in his language study.

He found what he was looking for in an American. But, alas, the man was a Christian missionary. Teikichi decided, though, that he could hurdle this obstacle by ignoring it and could capitalize on what he considered an excellent opportunity to learn to speak good English. And he accomplished his objective. How much this missionary influenced the later life of Teikichi is not known, but one cannot help believing that the Lord used His servant to pave the way for the young man's eventual conversion.

Teikichi made no outward move toward Christianity while in Japan. During his stay in Osaka, he adopted the theory of a friend that "man is all." While this philosophy tended to lead him away from his former Buddhist teachings, it certainly couldn't direct him toward the cross of Christ. Neither did it help him spiritually, for he found no relief for his emptiness of heart. Unable to understand this, he assumed he had not yet reached a sufficient level of temporal success to warrant it, so he drove himself to higher heights. He decided finally to go to America.

There, he reasoned, *his heart's desire would be fulfilled.*

As always, he laid his plans carefully. He asked his missionary friend scores of questions which covered the climate, the economy, the culture, the food. In short, he crossed every bridge he could think of before he purchased passage. Then he hired a tailor to make him a suit of clothes, and he bought an expensive leather bag. All this he did so that he might feel certain he would look prosperous and important in the strange land. There is little doubt he succeeded again in his objective.

His ambition carried him over the sea.

New World — New Life

It was midautumn, 1885. The morning sun rose above a rugged mountainous skyline, and projected great shafts of light through a bank of scraggly clouds, stippling the broad horizon with blazing color. A ship had just dropped anchor offshore at San Francisco, and scores of passengers lined the rails to view the miracle of dawn. To many of them — and to one, especially — it was a first introduction to the new world.

Teikichi Kawabe, restless and ambitious, but lonely

and depressed, gazed soberly at nature's gift-wrapped welcome to the Western world, unable to analyze his mixed emotions. He longed for material success and peace of heart. The first, he could manage; he was certain of that. But for all of his twenty-two years, the latter had been an elusive commodity he had never been able to call his own.

"I'll find it in America," he had promised himself again and again. But later that day as he walked the broad thoroughfares of San Francisco, he wondered whether he would ever enjoy the calm assurance he had sensed in the missionary friend who had taught him conversational English back in Tokyo. And, right then, he had to admit he was more thankful for that blessing than for all the others heaped together.

As he studied the drawn faces of the surging throng, he realized he was actually standing on the western rim of the world's great melting pot. Blue-eyed Saxons, dusky-skinned Latins, round-faced Polynesians, red men of America, black men of Africa, and Orientals, both like and unlike him, hurried through their workaday world. No one, not even a Japanese, paid any attention to him. By midafternoon, except in one small restaurant where he ate his first American meal, he had barely used his hard-earned English.

Toward evening, carrying his impressive leather bag, he made his way to a rather impressive-looking hotel. He was taken to the strangest room he had ever seen. It was large, light, and airy. A double bed, high off the floor and much too soft for comfort, was covered with a ridiculous patchwork quilt. On it were two great pillows stuffed with feathers which he feared might smother him in his sleep. On the floor, a thin, brightly flowered carpet was stretched taut to the walls, and, on a table in the corner stood a great white pitcher and bowl. On the wall hung the largest mirror he had ever seen. The next morning he found lodging in a Japanese rooming house, where he finally relaxed and felt very much at home.

In the 1880s, San Francisco was a bustling, frontier city, busy and dull by day, noisy and flashy by night, with more saloons and gambling dens than all other shops combined. Music — often tinny, always loud — filled the streets from dark to nearly dawn, as rough miners from the diggings and tough seamen from the docks drank, gambled, fought, and danced the hours away with professional "diggers" of another stripe. A man could be wealthy one moment, bankrupt the next, and dead, with a bullet through his temple before he left the gaming table. Money flowed from hand to hand with reckless abandon.

Teikichi Kawabe, who drank but never gambled, spent the dangerous nights alone in his room. But he was on the streets and in the shops by day, a legitimate man of business raking in the silver dollars, building himself an empire through which he sought in vain for peace.

By the time he was twenty-five, he had bartered and saved until he possessed enough funds to know that financial security alone held no answer to the spiritual problem that had plagued him all his life. But blind is the unregenerated heart, and simple logic alone fails miserably to convince the worldly mind of its error or cool the drive of an ambitious sinner. Something more earthshaking than any experience he had known was a prerequisite to his "coming to himself."

It came! The incident that finally brought Kawabe to his knees involved tragedy and heartbreak in the home of a special friend whose name was Miki Yamoto. Miki was an extremely successful man of business who had come to America penniless. In an amazingly short time he amassed a fortune, and by the time Teikichi, who was twenty years his junior, crossed his path, he was a millionaire with no limit to his desire for wealth and power.

Miki liked the young Kawabe whose ambitions matched his own, and his influence upon the younger man was probably greater than we can imagine. Miki Yamoto was a born enthusiast. No negative attitude or discouraging word ever marred his bubbling personality. His world was a happy, successful conquest that knew no sorrow nor defeat. He possessed the money to purchase whatever struck his fancy, and he thoroughly enjoyed the good life that he had carved out for himself and his family.

His pretty wife, Tomi, was unlike him in that the cold world of commerce and finance was distasteful to her sensitive soul. She enjoyed the security and easy life it provided — that was all. She admired her husband, whom she loved dearly, and upon him she was wholly, completely dependent. Tomi's interests were in the arts. She worked with oils and composed sonnets — an artist in her own right. Also she was a devoted mother of their only son, Miyake, a boy in early adolescence.

Miyake Yamoto was the proverbial "good boy" who resembled his mother in every respect. Whether the ambitious Miki was disappointed that his son did not share his talent in the business world was never known, for he too loved the boy with deep devotion, and he hoped to lay the world at his feet.

Teikichi was often in the Yamoto home, and here he saw everything he desired for himself. A fortune, a wife, a son, and nothing less than the great blue sky to place a limit upon his accomplishments.

Man is all, he reiterated. There was nothing in what he gazed upon that didn't please him. *This,* he mused, *is the life, and in it I shall find peace.*

How little did he realize the importance of that one word, *life* — life, only a heartbeat from eternity.

An epidemic of diphtheria invaded the city, and one of the first persons to contract the dread disease was Miyake Yamoto. In a few short days he was gone, leaving his loving parents alone in devastating sorrow. The grief-stricken couple leaned heavily upon Teikichi during the terrible days of their bereavement. His youth and his friendship became their strength.

After the burial, Miki called his young friend to him and said:

"My son, I have learned more during the past few days than I ever knew in all my life before. My sense of values has long been terribly distorted. When Miyake was trying to breathe his last breath, I realized that my money was as useless as the sands of the beach. I would gladly have given every penny of it — even to live in poverty the rest of my life — if only it would bring my boy back again.

"Tomi and I are selling out. I'm not sure where we will go or what we will do," he went on, "but we will always remember your kindness."

Teikichi started to answer him, but the older one gestured him to wait.

"My son," he said, "I haven't finished. Don't, please don't make the mistake that I have made. Try, if you can, to find a true sense of values and keep it always."

"Yes, sir," the young man answered. "Thank you, sir. I will, sir."

What happened to the Yamotos we do not know, for nothing further has been found concerning them.

For weeks the desperate young man walked the streets of San Francisco in a sort of dream. His world had crumbled at his feet. The elusive peace he had long been seeking seemed farther away than ever, and hardly a ray of hope was left.

He buried himself in his work and tried to forget his troubles. He even tried to enter into the revelry of the city's night life. But he found nothing to suggest that the empty void which enveloped body, mind, and spirit would ever be filled. Onward he trudged the lonely path, disturbed by his thoughts in the daytime, terrified by his dreams in the night, until he actually feared for his sanity.

But probably it was into such a low and devastating place as this that he had to wander before the Spirit of God could turn him around and lead him to victory. How long he wallowed in the slough of despair we do not know, but finally, like the prodigal in the field with the swine, he came to himself. He had to do something.

Along with all the iniquity those days, there was a lot of religion in the western metropolis. Buddhism, Shintoism, and various combinations of the two beckoned, especially to the Orientals. Teikichi had been down those roads before. But now, in his desperation, he was ready to seek for peace, even among the Christians whom he had long been taught to shun at any cost. Perhaps it was then that the kindly spirit of the missionary in Tokyo began to gnaw at his heart. Anyway, he was attracted to the soft strains of sacred music that reached him daily as he passed a Methodist mission, and one day he cautiously entered the open door. Kind missionaries witnessed to his hungry heart and presented the claims of Christ. For a time he pretended to be a Christian, trying to fool others as well as himself, but, of course, it was all to no avail. Then, finally, the devoted workers led him to the foot of the cross.

4

Adjustments

Startling changes in the thinking and, hence, in the life-style of persons saved out of darkness have, from the night of Nicodemus's visit with Jesus, been the hallmark of evangelical Christianity. These changes are as many and varied as the personalities they invade, and they constitute the dynamics in the Christian witness. The defeated alcoholic or hapless dope addict becomes a sober, sincere exponent of genuine Christian experience, and his testimony from the first bears fruit among his friends of former days.

No less startling is the adjustment in the behavior pattern of a converted "up and outer," and certainly no less effective is his witness at his end of the socioeconomic ladder.

Greater evidence of this can hardly be found than in the conversion of Teikichi Kawabe, the extroverted, temperate, well-groomed, successful businessman, whose "Midas touch" had been recognized quickly by the titans of commerce in the bustling city of San Francisco. Not that the young man lost the "Midas touch" when he accepted Christ, but the extreme importance of financial security that had dominated his life from the time he was a boy, dimmed completely in the pure light of the gospel.

He accepted without question a new sense of security that involved eternal life. He experienced a new drive — the winning of souls — as the making of money suddenly appeared cheap and worldly to him. In his new life-style, money became a medium of exchange — something to trade for the necessities of life. He could hardly have cared less whether he received remuneration for his work in kingdom building. He knew he was capable of repairing his finances when the necessity arose. *After all,* he reasoned, *didn't the Apostle Paul step out of harness upon occasion to make tents, supporting not only himself but others who labored with him?*

In his zeal for the work, however, Teikichi seldom exercised this prerogative, and there were times when poverty stalked his steps as he pressed forward with the gospel of Christ. He never complained.

An old Japanese proverb, "When a boy goes out of his

own country, there are problems everywhere," had been real — too real — in Teikichi's life in America. Only with his conversion did the problems melt away. His acceptance of Christ as Saviour came on the last Thursday of November 1887, which was America's Thanksgiving Day, and thankful indeed was the heart of Teikichi Kawabe. "The time for celebrating *eternity* has come to me," he said. And years later, when describing his conversion, he wrote, "I experienced an X ray from heaven which shined into my heart. The words of John 16:8, 'And when he is come, he will reprove the world of sin, and of righteousness, and of judgment,' suddenly exposed the things in my heart that until now had been hidden. All my innermost secrets were exposed, and the truth of God was shown to me. Those things I did not want to see I had to face — even my most hideous sins and my awful condition I was made to know.

"I was the worst of sinners," he went on, "a hypocritical Pharisee, a cursed sinner. For the first time in my life, before God I was ashamed, and with tears I confessed my sins, repented, and worshiped the Lord of the cross. From my heart, I believed in Jesus as my Saviour and received forgiveness. I heard the Lord say to me, 'My child, rest, for I have forgiven your sins . . . and you have become a child of God.'

"This assurance was clearly given to me. My salvation had come, not by my good works, but by my faith only in the Lord. I knew my sins were all forgiven, and I had become God's child. I could not refrain from giving vent to tears of joy. Hallelujah!"

Brother Kawabe (as we shall call him hereafter), in speaking of his conversion, always made his testimony explicit by using pointed illustrations from his personal experience. For example, on one occasion he said, "When God forgave me of my sins, He also healed my sinful relationship with other people." Again he told of a young man by the name of Yomakoshi with whom he had crossed the ocean. In America, they had each invested $2.55 in a razor which was a valuable commodity in those early days.

"But," Brother Kawabe explained years later, "I took the razor and did not reimburse my friend."

He went on to explain that, even though it was a very small thing, the Lord brought it to his remembrance following his conversion, so he went to Yomakoshi and paid him for it. He was hesitant at first, he said, when the Lord required him to make restitution, but greater peace was added to him when he finally obeyed.

Less than a month following his conversion, Brother Kawabe, along with a man named Kanzo Uchimura, who likewise became an outstanding Christian leader, was baptized by Bishop Harris and joined the Methodist church.

Then, sometime in the months that followed, there came a day when Brother Kawabe, happy as he was in his new experience, discovered it was difficult to commit the good things in life — as well as the bad — to the whole will of God. He sensed, vaguely at first, that a closer relationship with Christ was somehow imperative, but just how to enter into it was both confusing and disturbing to his sensitive heart.

By the following summer, he had become miserable in his conviction. Then, as he often explained later with great emphasis, he found the answer to his problem when a friend with whom he studied in seminary told of fasting and praying over a similar, if not identical, burden. The friend went on to say that, one day, he experienced what he believed was a new baptism — not of water, but of fire — which he felt had cleansed his heart and filled his life with greater joy and a power to witness more effectively than he had ever known. He finished with an earnestness he had never displayed before, exhorting all his friends to seek the baptism of the Holy Spirit.

Brother Kawabe testified many times throughout his life that he was so stirred by his friend's exhortation that for eight days he sought the whole will of God, trying desperately to place his life, his talents, his money, his time, *his all* on an altar of sacrifice.

His call to preach came early in his Christian life. This was no small thing for his conscientious heart to accept, and the awesome responsibility that accompanied it was nearly overwhelming. He had to be sure. His fear of Satan was as strong as his faith in God, and lest his impressions be coming from the enemy appearing as an angel of light, he went into seclusion for an extended period of fasting and prayer.

"I became very humble," he wrote, "and I was filled with deep emotion. I left association with others to give myself to prayer and Bible reading only. I said to myself," he continued, *"If I am not filled with the Holy Spirit, I cannot work for God. I would rather die!"*

For two long months he refused to admit his friends. Even his mail, including letters from home, lay unopened until the day he came forth from his hermitage, aglow with that peace of God that passeth all understanding.

Then he preached. Rooted in his heart, nourished in his breast, was the message of salvation that gushed from his lips with neither fear nor favor. And few indeed were the hungry hearts that could resist it.

His testimony regarding his full commitment to Christ never failed to stir hearts. "It came," he said, "on the seventh day of August, 1889, for which I am deeply grateful . . . .

"Until that time, I had been a believer for a year and eight months," he explained. "During that time I had sinned and repented over and over again. By natural disposition it was easy for me to become angry and thus to sin readily. When I did this, I repented before God and made things right with men, but from this constant sinning and repenting I was unable to escape."

"One thing I noticed during those months was that I boasted in myself, but when I surrendered my life, counting it as nothing, I John 1:17 was applied to my heart."

Brother Kawabe testified in later life that, following his conversion, he felt the call of God to be an evangelist, but it was not until he made a full commitment to Christ that he was willing to say yes to the call.

The most noticeable change in Brother Kawabe following his conversion was in his attitudes, his ambitions, and his affections. No one who knew him ever doubted that he came soon to the place of *love made perfect*. He loved God supremely, more than self in every area of his life, and for nearly fifty years he was never known to falter in his walk with the Lord.

Family ties are important in most parts of the world, but they are extremely so in Japanese culture. Not for a moment did Brother Kawabe forget his family in Japan, and an overwhelming burden for their souls settled down upon him following his conversion. He wrote home immediately, explaining in the best way he could the joy and peace he experienced in salvation. He sent a Bible, not knowing how it would be accepted. With it went his most earnest prayers.

The Holy Spirit was faithful at the other end of the line, for Seizaburo Kawabe, the father of the family, was so impressed by his son's earnest testimony that he set aside his prejudices enough, at least, to read aloud from the Bible each day to his loved ones.

It should be noted here that, later, when Brother Kawabe arrived back in Japan, he went at once to his father's house. Seizaburo had always been fond of wine, and he drank it regularly, often to excess. Following his son's visit, however, he became a total abstainer, and later he stated that the promise of Acts 16:31, "Believe on the Lord Jesus Christ, and thou shalt be saved, and thy house," became his promise too, for *he was a believer.*"

Missionary to Japan

Brother Kawabe worked with the Methodist mission in San Francisco where he had become a member. His effectiveness in soul winning never ceased to amaze his colleagues who, being much better trained than he, were not doing nearly as well. This is not to say that training is not important, but rather that the enthusiasm and emotional appeal of a newborn Christian, aglow with his first love, is best described as "a flame of living fire."

It was during this period that he met and won the homesick lad, Yosuke Matsuoka, whose story was told in chapter one.

In January 1894, nine years after his arrival in America, Brother Kawabe was engaged in a season of intense, intercessory prayer for a friend in Japan. In telling the incident later, he said he heard the clear call of the Lord to *go*. Whether this was an impression or the audible voice of God is not clear, but, in any event, he was certain it meant for him to carry the gospel back to Japan. This was most confusing to him, for he had no funds, no backing, and no ordination, the latter being of utmost importance to the Japanese. He waited upon the Lord, for his faith was strong that patience and trust were always rewarded by heaven, and in less than a month he found that it was so.

In February he accompanied a friend named Sasao Tetsusaburo across the bay to Oakland to attend an

Alliance meeting in which missionary work was considered paramount in Christian service. Ministers were being ordained, to "go . . . into all the world and preach the gospel."

Brother Kawabe had given himself to a much more intense theological study than anyone realized. Hence, it was with faith and assurance that he presented himself as a candidate for ordination. He amazed his interrogators with profound insights into the Word.

So it happened that Teikichi Kawabe, proudly carrying his precious parchment, left the Methodist church and began to evangelize up and down the coast with neither denominational backing nor financial support. He could have taken time off to work and replenish his bank account, but he felt the "woe" to preach, and sure enough, his every need was met as he pursued his arduous schedule.

This, he reasoned well, was the answer to the problem he faced in accepting his call to Japan. Faith and obedience were the dollars and cents that would keep bread upon the table and a roof above his head.

So, in typical Kawabe fashion, he laid his plans with great care and dispatch and landed in Yokohama on March 19, 1895. Following his fruitful visit to the parental home, he took lodging in an inexpensive inn and then went into the mountains alone to pray. It was there, he related fifty years later, he received the assurance from heaven that he was on the right road. Those early days of his ministry in Japan were precious and enlightening.

The weather was warm and sunny as the month of May ushered in the unusually pleasant summer of 1895. Flowers bloomed beautifully, and a gentle ocean breeze from over the bay warmed the hearts of the people as Brother Kawabe walked down a street in the teeming city of Osaka. He was told that more than 600 thousand souls lived in at least 115 thousand dwellings in this metropolis. Few had heard the good news of salvation. His work was laid out for him; of that much he was sure.

It is true that by 1895 there were missionaries on the islands, representing various churches and independent mission boards across the sea, but nearly all of them had settled in the larger Tokyo area. Osaka had been bypassed and was practically destitute of the gospel.

By the first of June, Brother Kawabe had succeeded in rounding up eight persons who had had some contact with Christianity. He met with them regularly, witnessing always to the saving grace of God through Jesus Christ. Then imitating the Apostle Paul, who never failed to put his converts to work as soon as he had trained them sufficiently, Brother Kawabe organized his little band of eight (nine counting himself), and through the months of June, July, and August, they distributed tracts to every home in the city. Since they limited this ministry to half days, each worker reached an average of more than one hundred doors each morning for that entire period. But that was not all. In the afternoons they conducted evangelistic services, first in a rented house and later in an old theater building which they were able to lease.

We have no statistical report of how successful this three-month ministry proved to be, but we know that the laborers were happy with it and decided to move on to other areas to follow the same pattern.

Their first move was to Nara Prefecture, where they teamed up with another evangelist named Yoshigoro Akiyama. In a comparatively short time they covered the city of Nara with tracts.

Up to this point their labors had been confined to areas in which the Christian religion had at least been introduced. Now they decided to go to the city of Iga, where 100 thousand people living in 20 thousand homes had never heard the name of Jesus. In all probability this was a period of seed sowing rather than harvesting, but there must have been enough interest aroused to keep the faithful witnesses about their Master's business.

After the tract campaign in Iga, Brother Kawabe went to the island of Awaji, an area that was to test his mettle and where, indeed, he nearly gave up in despair. It was at Fukura on Awaji Island that he met an old friend, Seiji Kakihara, who had been a student of his in San Francisco.

Mr. Kakihara had been laboring there for a year, a missionary representing the Free Methodist Church of North America. Since he had met with little or no success in Fukura, he had already made plans to leave, "shaking the dust from his feet." He had great confidence, though, in his former teacher, and he was anxious that he take over the responsibilities of the field.

"If anyone can break through the walls of indifference in Fukura," he said, "it surely will be you, Brother Kawabe."

But Brother Kawabe was not convinced that he should labor again under the wing of an established denomination. He enjoyed his work as an independent evangelist. However, Seiji Kakihara was a most persuasive fellow and refused to take no for an answer. He wrote at once to the General Missionary Board in Chicago, and as a result Teikichi Kawabe was accepted and appointed as a missionary of the Free Methodist Church. As such, he labored for more than half a century with unprecedented success. Eventually he built up and pastored the largest congregation in the entire denomination, Nipponbashi, Osaka.

But success did not come quickly. The people of Awaji Island were cold and indifferent — sometimes hostile and defensive — to the evangelistic efforts of Brother Kawabe. There were times when discouragement nearly defeated him. It seemed that nothing would work. Regardless of how effective a method had been on earlier occasions, he was unable to use it in Fukura to reach the hearts of the people. They refused to attend services no matter how carefully planned and well publicized they were, and he felt certain the tracts he distributed daily were carelessly discarded, unheeded and unread.

So he searched for some new method of reaching the people. *Where,* he asked himself, *do the people gather regularly, that I might gain their attention?*

Then one day the answer to his question came. *The public bathhouse! Yes, yes, that is where I shall reach the people,* he must have said.

In any event, it was outside the public bathhouse that he took his stand, witnessing, preaching, counseling, weeping until one day, December 31, 1897, he saw his first sinner converted.

This was the beginning, for then he had the fresh, unvarnished testimony of a babe in Christ to document his message. Slowly but surely the tiny seeds he had been planting began to take root. Then God used another, a non-Christian young nurse, to spread the news of Brother Kawabe's effectual, fervent prayers. Her words were heeded by all who heard her tell of the amazing miracles of faith she had witnessed, especially the healing of Brother Kawabe's small son who had been given up to die.

Brother Kawabe had married an excellent helpmeet, a beautiful, talented lady named Ryuko Sumika. Strangely enough, she was an extremely extroverted, athletic girl. This, of course, was hardly in the Japanese tradition, but it was said that never was any note of resentment voiced by her peers. She was deeply spiritual and was loved by everyone.

Ryuko had an older sister, the wife of a Christian businessman in Osaka, who later became an Episcopal priest. It was through this family that she was introduced to Christianity and made her commitment to Christ. She attended the Shoan Girls' Mission School in Osaka where she was baptized.

Then there came the day that she heard Brother Kawabe preaching under the anointing of the Holy Spirit. She was so impressed that she arranged to meet him.

Eventually they married, and each of them lived to be ninety years of age. Their life together was a delightful experience, and to this union were born two children, a son and a daughter. The son, after his miraculous healing, grew to manhood and became an excellent minister in his own right. He died several years ago. His sister is still living.

 A Changing Country

Japan is an ever-changing country, and to understand the culture and habits of the people of more than eighty-five years ago, when Brother Kawabe returned home with the gospel, it is necessary for us to read from someone who wrote about Japan at that particular time.

So we are inserting here an article entitled "Social Life in Japan," by Mrs. Yo Uchida, wife of the Japanese counsul. The article appeared in *Collier's Weekly* about the turn of the century. Even then, as we learn from Mrs. Uchida's first paragraph, changes were coming fast to the islands of Japan. She wrote as follows:

> With ever-increasing interest, I read Western books and magazine articles about my own country, but I find that many of them are very incorrect in their descriptions of Japanese life and customs. During the last thirty years, or within a single generation, the customs and manners of my people have changed very greatly. This has been brought about by the

introduction and ready acceptance by us of Western civilization. But the transformation is not yet complete. Japanese life, as reflected in its customs and manners, is still in a state of transition. Those who visited our country under the old regime could hardly have imagined that in so short a time railways and telegraph lines would be extended into almost every part of the island, that electric lights would illumine the cities of the Mikado as they do the capitals of Europe and the great cities of the United States, that telephones would be in use everywhere, that buildings of Western architecture would be too common to attract attention, and that almost every advanced idea of the Western World would find immediate acceptance in the island empire.

Along with these changes in public and business life have come, also, tremendous and necessary changes in our social and family life. Some of our people now live exactly as you do in this country — dwelling in homes built according to Western ideas, wearing the Western style of dress, and eating food of the kind preferred in the West and cooked in Western ways. They give receptions, entertainments in their homes, dinners, balls, and all other social functions in the strictest manner of the West. But there are others who cling halfheartedly to the old manners and customs. These live in a style that is half Western and half Eastern — half European and half Japanese. This class marks the intermediate stage bewteen the old regime and the new. Almost all of the common-class people, however, still live in the old fashion. The few changes they have adopted in their dress and style of living only serve to accentuate the more the peculiarities of both civilizations.

In Japan the center of social life is the family. Every one is supposed to belong to some family and to be attached to its residence. The family is more closely united than it is in America, for there are no tenement and apartment houses in my country. Each family occupies its own home, however humble it may be. A Japanese house for a middle class family usually consists of from seven to ten rooms, with a little garden attached. Besides the married couple and their children, some of their relatives usually live in the same house — their brothers, sisters, and parents being entitled to membership in the same family. An important feature in our home life is that younger members of the family must pay special respect to the elder members. This practice extends to brothers and sisters as well as to children of the household. The head of the family is usually a married man, who is responsible for the support of the entire household and for the management of the estate. According to our customs, property was formerly considered as belonging to the family instead of to the individual and stood in the names of the ''heads'' of families. This has been changed, however, and by recent laws any person in Japan, male or female, may now own property in his or her individual right. But all property of the family is still transferred from head to head, whenever there is a change in the headship. It is partly due to this custom that our people are especially solicitous about the perpetuation of the family. If there are no children, a boy or youth from another family is adopted, and he succeeds in due time to the headship.

About the same time that Mrs. Uchida was writing the above article, attempting to set her American friends straight regarding her country, there was published by *Gospel in All Lands,* the following ''Japanese Ten Commandments'':

1. Be loyal to the Sovereign, filial to parents, and reverence Divine Beings.
2. Respect the Imperial Family and love your country.
3. Observe the law of your country and strive to promote the national interests.
4. Study hard in the pursuance of knowledge and be mindful of health.
5. Devote the best efforts to your profession or avocation.
6. Make a peaceful home and love your neighbors.
7. Be faithful and benevolent.
8. Take care not to injure others' interests. Practice charity.
9. Do not indulge in the pleasures of drinking and debauchery. Make not unjust gains.
10. As to religion, you may believe in any you choose but be careful to avoid one that is injurious to the interests of your country.

Since the youngsters of one generation become the adults of the next, it may help us to understand the Japanese people among whom Brother Kawabe evangelized at the height of his ministry, by looking closely at the children of thirty years before. The following excerpts are from an article that appeared in an early issue of the *Missionary Tidings*. The author's name was not given.

The child of Dai Nippon goes not only to school, but to the family temple also, where the prayers he offers are very poetical. He pulls the cord that sounds the gong, claps his chubby brown hands together to call the attention of the god to his petitions, clasps his fingers under his chin, then repeats his prayer. Mayhap an old woman is seated at the door of the sanctuary with a cage of birds before her. As a child passes he gives her a small sum of money, perhaps not more than a rin, which is equal to one-tenth of a cent, in return for which a captive bird is set free. (The teaching is that in this way, the child sets some lost soul free to reach Nirvana — the Buddhist heaven.)

Then, too, children are taken on long pilgrimages to some famous temple or shrine . . . .

It is common to see a group of boys and girls before the carved doors, with the father or an old priest explaining the significance of the marvelous figures.

A favorite subject is "The Monkeys of India, China, and Japan," which adorn the alcoves. Every child knows that the covering of eyes, mouth, and ears, means the monkeys see no evil, speak no evil, hear no evil.

There is something very solemn about a Japanese temple, and the grounds are an extraordinary sight. One can get tea at the numerous booths along the way and purchase rice and beans for offerings to the gods. The latter may be designated as the "sacred white horse," an albino pony, a greedy little creature with pink eyes, that grows fat at the expense of small children.

The everyday life of the common people is interesting. They rise early, fold their quilts, and put away their little wooden or bamboo pillows. This kind of pillow was imperative for boys as well as girls on account of the elaborate dressing of the hair. Now the boys wear their hair cut after the American fashion.

It is especially amusing to watch the children use their chopsticks, although they are exceedingly dexterous in handling the little instruments. They are made of bamboo, mahogany, or ivory and are held in various ways just as American boys and girls hold their knives and forks in different positions. The better class of people never use the same chopsticks twice.

Perhaps most interesting of all is a letter which was written in 1898 by Sister Kawabe, addressed to Mrs. Winget. It reads:

I would like to write a long letter to you, but I am not able to do so, for my baby takes my attention. When we came to Fukura last June, the Sunday school was very small — only fifteen or twenty children. By the help of God, the school has grown every week. Now I have nearly one hundred children. I think some of them are truly converted by their lives. Their parents are much moved. Many of them are praying daily in their houses. Most of them can recite Scripture passages.

I have another school in Shijuki, but it is inconvenient for me to go. At present Mr. Kawabe teaches school whenever he is there. Please pray for these children, that they may become shining lights in their heathen families; also pray for me that I may not disturb his good work which has begun among them. I am sending pictures of them and others. Much love to you and Mr. Winget.

R. KAWABE

A pamphlet written by missionary Anna Youngren about 1920 included the following paragraph which further documents the success enjoyed by Brother Kawabe.

At Takasago, on the Banshu District, the chief of police, who has been interested for some time, was clearly converted at a recent meeting held by Mr. Kawabe. He was so deeply in earnest that he requested baptism at once, and accordingly he was baptized in the river at eleven o'clock the same night. His joy is unbounded over his new experience.

7

Loyal Free Methodist

At once, Brother Kawabe found peace and genuine satisfaction in his new relationship with the Free Methodist Church, for in both doctrine and practice it paralleled his most earnest convictions. Many years later, after he had become an old man he continued to stand by the old landmarks. We unearthed and have had translated into English the following paragraphs from his pen:

The tradition which the Free Methodist Association has received includes perfect salvation, perfect cleansing. Regardless of what may happen, these two experiences which are received by faith alone, we must guard tenaciously. Our church in America has earnestly contended for these two truths. And over the past fifty years of our history in Japan, the same has been true in our evangelical ministry . . . .

And now the necessity of evangelism: salvation, holiness, the Second Coming, healing, and the supplying of our financial needs; from these fundamentals we must never move. Everyone must hold to them tenaciously. Further, we must pass them on to the next generation. I exhort with all my heart that we do this. These are my parting words to you.

41

These words were read by Brother Kawabe on the occasion of the fiftieth anniversary of the Free Methodist Fellowship in Japan.

So when he began work within the denomination, his former desire to labor as an independent evangelist was lost forever. He discovered soon that denominational backing added strength to the truth he was preaching, and the prayers of hundreds of Christians in America gave power to his message. Third in importance, but no less appreciated, was the financial assistance he received from abroad.

The pattern of his ministry was well established, and he intended to follow it for life. Then, alas, an unexpected letter from the missionary secretary in Chicago almost defeated his purpose. The letter came as a result of an economic depression, which hit the nation suddenly and with such impact that, naturally, missionary giving dropped off considerably.

The letter was brief. It stated simply that there were no funds available for the Japanese work, and no change for the better was anticipated in the foreseeable future. Therefore, the board was recommending Brother Kawabe to the Alliance people in Hiroshima, and it was their earnest prayer that, in this new situation, he would be used of God in the salvation of souls. They were sorry.

The letter was a cruel blow, especially since it followed the breakthrough for which the Kawabes had labored and prayed so long. It was not intentional, of course, for the missionary secretary was not aware of the progress being made, and he did have to cut expenses wherever possible. Brother Kawabe doubted none of this, but nonetheless the letter came as a stab in the heart. He was unable to understand it.

"Why?" he cried. "Why would heaven permit so devastating a setback at such a strategic time to go forward with the gospel?" Yet his good sense told him that he dare not blame God. He knew that somewhere there had to be both a reason and an answer. Of one thing he was sure: He would not turn his back on the field he had opened, nor on the church that could no longer afford his services. He would continue to labor and build under the banner of the Free Methodist Church, depending wholly upon God to supply the necessary funds.

It wasn't easy then, but now one can see the hand of God at work. The same Christ who had led His little band of disciples through three years of intensive training, involving hardship, persecution, and overwhelming disappointment was leading Teikichi Kawabe down the same rough road. The old trail was still there, unimproved, but out of the last valley the dreary way cut sharply upward to where the sun broke through the mists, and victory blazed across the noonday sky.

The first year as an "independent Free Methodist" Brother Kawabe suffered every hardship, endured every disappointment, and resisted every temptation conceivable. He wrote about it as follows:

> I had evangelized at Fukura on Awaji; the gospel was being preached; and all of this was not the result of my thinking or planning. Thus, until God's clear voice could be heard, I could not go elsewhere as the General Missionary Board had suggested. I prayed earnestly and looked to the Lord for guidance. Thus I remained in this place and evangelized. The person who is obedient to God's will must be prepared for this necessity. I believed God and went on from there.

But "on from there" was not as simple as it sounds. He had to have workers, and there was no place to get them except from the ranks of his own converts. As always, it was true that a small percentage of them felt the divine call to special Christian service, but they had to be trained. He had no choice but to establish a school in which to prepare them for the work ahead. This was the first step of faith he took, following the heartbreaking news from America. He had to have money, for, as he said in one of his papers, "Already, because several persons were engaged in evangelism, every month 150 yen was necessary."

After promising the Lord that he would do everything possible to answer his own prayers and then depend upon heaven for the rest, he searched in vain for a part-time job which he could handle along with his heavy responsibilities. In a noble effort to meet current expenses (he refused to go into debt), he began to sell his precious books. Finally he sold his typewriter.

His loyal wife, Ryuko, made lace which he sold in the city of Kobe. Then she taught the lady evangelists to make lace too. Finally Brother Kawabe found congenial employment teaching English to the military police. The young men who were studying in the seminary he had set up, worked part of each day in the fields for the farmers. By the end of the year, the missionary enterprise was solvent and very much alive. Not only that, but souls were being saved, and the work showed healthy growth. Brother Kawabe, up before the dawn, prayed and praised the Lord without ceasing.

It has been said that nothing in this world succeeds as well as success itself. Brother Kawabe and his loyal followers were soon to learn that the strange maxim was true, although they were completely unaware of what was taking place far from Awaji Island and Fukura.

Benjamin Winget, general missionary secretary from Chicago, visited the struggling work in China. While there he met a man who had just arrived from Japan. The two shared news from their respective countries. The Japanese gentleman boasted that he had many friends on the west coast of America, and Mr. Winget replied that he had a good friend in Japan, a minister by the name of

Teikichi Kawabe.

"Kawabe!" his new friend exploded. "I know Kawabe. I saw him not more than a month ago in the city of Kobe, selling his books to carry on his school. I heard later he is doing an excellent work on Awaji Island for the Free Methodist Church."

Winget could hardly believe his ears, for he was under the impression that the Free Methodist work was closed. Immediately he altered his schedule in order to stop over in Japan on his homeward journey.

When Mr. Winget finally reached Fukura, Kawabe and his friends welcomed him with open arms. They expressed their grief over the problems that were afflicting the church in America.

"We cannot move forward as speedily as we would like," Brother Kawabe told him, "but the Lord is blessing our efforts. Someday we will have the money for the things we need to evangelize effectively."

To say there was no end to Winget's amazement would be putting it mildly. He returned to America with a new story to tell.

The result was that the Missionary Board adjusted whatever funds were at its disposal and sent a wholly new and different letter to Brother Kawabe, congratulating him on his faithful service and unprecedented success. Then, the letter informed him that once again financial assistance would be coming regularly from America.

We can hardly imagine the rejoicing at the little seminary when that letter was read. It contained about the best news Brother Kawabe ever heard, not because of the money, but because God had vindicated His promise. All things *were* working together for good to them that love Him.

During that year of extreme hardship, the faithful missionary and his people had learned their greatest lessons. The inspiration received was of far greater worth than the money, and their faith in God so increased that their future success came almost as a matter of course.

Brother Kawabe never changed his position or compromised his ideals. Nearly half a century later he wrote, "Whether in sickness or financial difficulty, we must evangelize. We must evangelize even unto death if necessary. For this purpose we must rely upon God's Word with all our hearts. We must be ready to expose our hearts completely to God and be intimately related to Him. We must believe in the power of prayer. Therefore, every day we must die, and by the power of the Holy Spirit, live in Christ."

Following his reinstatement as a bona fide missionary of the Free Methodist Church, Brother Kawabe and his loyal workers went to work with greater zeal than ever. An excerpt from a letter which he wrote about that time to the missionary secretary reads as follows:

Since January two backsliders came back to their Heavenly Father and got a deeper and higher experience than ever before, and many new inquirers have accepted Christ as their own Saviour. Some of them were soundly converted, and others were healed of sickness of body by faith. He is indeed faithful to His Word. Praise God for His wonderful work of love. And still pray for those probationers . . . and also for the people who are still in the darkness of heathenism in this town and vicinity. . . .

BROTHER KAWABE

With the work moving along well in Fukura, a burden for the teeming thousands of souls in Osaka settled upon the hearts of the Kawabes, and it became the heart cry in all their prayers.

The Kawabes had this photo taken ''in grateful memory of our visit to America.''

Dr. Tetsuji Tsuchiyama and family in 1920. He became superintendent of the Japan Conference when Brother Kawabe resigned.

The Kawabes, Christmas 1940

The first seminary building in Osaka, erected in 1922

The first mission home, left, and girls' dorm, destroyed in World War II

The college and seminary campus was completely destroyed during World War II. Thinking it a factory complex, it was bombed three times by the American Air Force.

Nipponbashi church, damaged by fire bombs in 1945 — the only building in the area that remained standing

The Kawabes, 1951. He was eighty-eight and she was seventy-seven.

The library, the newest building on the present Osaka Christian College campus

Dr. Kaneo Oda (in 1952), first General Superintendent (Bishop) of the Japan General Conference

The Reverend T. Uzaki, present General Superintendent (Bishop) of the Japan General Conference

8

Osaka

Leaving the Fukura church in good hands, Brother Kawabe — in the pattern established by Paul — moved on to other fields. Hence, we find him evangelizing in the city of Osaka in the early spring of 1903.

His excellent wife, Ryuko, was a most efficient helper. Not only was she gifted with a beautiful soprano voice which she dedicated wholly to the Lord, but her ability to speak and teach English was an invaluable asset to her husband's ministry. One of her students became the mayor of Tokyo, and another became president of Hosei University. For twenty-five years, she taught a Bible class at her husband's church, with as many as 120 women in attendance. Twice during her lifetime she visited America.

The year 1903 was an excellent time for the Kawabes to begin their work in Osaka. An all-Japan exposition was in progress in the Tennoji area of the city, and there they ministered to great numbers of people every day.

Interest and response were exceptionally good, but how to follow up converts at a mammoth fair with thousands of people moving here and there presented a difficult problem. To simply ignore it would be equivalent to a mother ignoring her newborn babe. Babes in Christ and babes in arms need constant loving care, and Brother Kawabe did not want to let his converts die for lack of nourishment and protection.

He found a house for rent near Tanamizu Bashi. There was no way of knowing then whether he could establish a church in a dwelling, but he hoped to use the building as a type of counseling center, a place to which he would direct his converts and others who were showing interest in the gospel. He took a short-time lease on the property, hurriedly equipped it the best he could to serve his purpose, and invited the people to meet him there at certain hours. He wondered whether any would appear.

He didn't wonder long. The people came — first a few, then more and more until the facility was packed. Fortunately, he was able to rent the place next door. Apparently these residences were joined together, for years later Brother Kawabe wrote that by knocking out a partition between the two houses, a much larger area in which to hold services was possible. The work went well, and soon this facility was inadequate too. The experiment, however, taught the ambitious missionary two important facts. First, the people were in earnest in their desire to learn more about God, and second, the establishment of a permanent place of worship was necessary to the continuing success of the venture. But the financing of such a project was not yet realistic.

The next step was to open a large evangelistic hall — another temporary measure. Although this hall provided sufficient room to accommodate great congregations, the atmosphere produced by the stark, boxlike structure was hardly conducive to the best in spiritual worship. However, Kawabe's fervent preaching and effectual praying, along with Mrs. Kawabe's quiet counseling and behind-the-scenes ministry, overcame this obstacle until they were able to move their congregation to a satisfactory church plant at Nipponbashi.

As John Wesley told his preachers they had nothing to do but save souls, so pastoring, teaching, and building the Nipponbashi congregation was central in Brother Kawabe's labors of love — a ministry that involved every facet of evangelism and every area of Christian service. As the church grew, he established outposts which he called evangelistic halls. These preaching points were extensions of the main church, and it is amazing to see how the Free Methodist work suddenly began to grow.

In October 1903, the outreach ministry began in earnest with an evangelistic point created at Sumoto. Exactly one year later, October 1904, another hall was established at Shimodera Machi; in 1907 still another appeared at Akashi, and others followed. Finally, it became evident that Brother Kawabe had founded the largest Free Methodist church in the world. Also, it was the largest Christian congregation in the city, as the following excerpt from a paper written at that time relates:

> The Osaka church [Nipponbashi] now has the largest regular congregation of any church in the city and has become a strong religious center. An early Saturday morning prayer meeting has been conducted by Pastor Kawabe for years, the special object of which has been to pray for revival. A number of the young men belonging to the Evangelistic Band of the Osaka church have prayed all night. Such praying always brings results. One young apprentice spent all night in prayer with the result that his employer, who was already a Christian, got under deep conviction, rededicated himself to God, and decided to give one-tenth of his income to the Lord. One profligate young man who had embezzled funds from his employer attempted at three different times to drown himself in Osaka harbor. He was providentially led to one of the chapels where he was marvelously converted.

By the time World War I was winding down in 1918, the whole world was undergoing great changes, and leaders of missionary movements everywhere were preparing for unprecedented advance. The Free Methodist Church, which had become progressively missionary minded, was a small denomination, but in the Osaka area of Japan it was the best known of all Protestant churches.

Free Methodism was almost synonymous with Protestantism. The reason, as suggested earlier, was that all other groups had established their headquarters in the Tokyo area.

In 1921 a Japanese Free Methodist Conference was initiated, and Brother Kawabe became the superintendent. Leading up to this dramatic step in the work, it had become evident that a much too heavy load was being placed upon the shoulders of this one man. It was then that the church leaders in America began to seek for a well-trained missionary/educator to assist him.

The man for the hour was a Japanese-born, highly trained man, who like Brother Kawabe had gone to America to get rich and there had found the riches of God in Christ Jesus. This man, who later was to become well known in Free Methodist missionary circles, was Tetsuji Tsuchiyama. Tsuchiyama was graduated from a Christian college in Pasadena, California, then went on to complete the three-year course at Drew Theological Seminary. Later, he received a master's degree in theology at Princeton, after which he went to Palestine to do further research. Still later he was awarded the doctor of divinity degree from his alma mater.

Tetsuji Tsuchiyama joined the Free Methodist Church in 1917 and accepted an offer from the Missionary Board to go to Osaka as soon as his seminary training at Drew was completed. He was to relieve Brother Kawabe of his school responsibility, and assist generally in the work. This he did. It was some time later that he returned to America for further training.

Brother Kawabe had established the first Free Methodist school in Osaka for the training of evangelists. It developed into what is now Osaka Christian College. It is doubtful that any pioneer missionary ever sensed the need for sound academic training for the men and women who were called of God to Christian service more than did

Teikichi Kawabe, although he was not specially trained in that field. Beginning with what he called a theological seminary on Awaji Island, his influence has been felt in every step the church in Japan has taken in the field of education from that moment to this. Osaka Christian College with an enrollment of more than twelve hundred and also a school of theology are operating presently in Osaka, reflecting his farsightedness.

However, Kawabe was not an educator in the same sense and degree as was Tetsuji Tsuchiyama, who assumed direction of the school. The former planted, watered, and cultivated; Tsuchiyama took over and finally reaped the harvest. Both men served in their own way and time with great distinction. Tsuchiyama was welcomed to Japan by Brother Kawabe, and immediately the administration of the school in Osaka was his.

During his first year back in Japan, Tsuchiyama supplied the Nipponbashi church while Brother Kawabe took a year off to visit America again and pursue further study on his own. When he returned to Japan, the two men agreed that both the location and the buildings of the School for Evangelists were inadequate, and a determined search for something better began. There was a small park for sale just outside the city, which the men were able to purchase, and a building program was soon underway. Eventually classrooms, chapel, dining area, a publishing house, two dormitories, and four teachers' residences were completed. Osaka was growing, and soon the city surrounded the school. Today one can hardly believe it ever stood out in the country.

In 1922 the name of the school was changed to Japan Free Methodist Seminary, and an entrance requirement — completion of middle school, eleventh year — was established. Before that, the only requirement for registration was to be ''called'' to evangelism.

By then, the church in America had for some time

been sending missionaries to assist in the work. In a group photograph of the first annual conference of the Japan Free Methodist Church (1923) are pictured Lillian Pickens, Gertrude Aylard, Minnie K. Hessler, the Reverend and Mrs. H. H. Wagner, the Reverend and Mrs. Roy Millikan, and the Reverend and Mrs. W. B. Olmstead. Mr. Olmstead was then the general missionary secretary of the church.

During the remainder of the 1920s, the Free Methodist Church in Japan continued to grow under the spiritual, aggressive leadership of Brother Kawabe assisted by his good companion and by the ever-growing number of workers from both home and abroad. As superintendent of the work, Kawabe traveled from one area to another, preaching, counseling, organizing as the work progressed. The Tokyo area was entered in cooperation with other Protestant groups. Free Methodist congregations were gradually established there.

The Stormy Thirties

The year 1930 dawned with dark forebodings. By then a mighty nation with an exploding population was crowded into an extremely small territory, and further conquest by Japan was thought inevitable. War with nearby China threatened. The man on the street, the woman in the home, even the child in school sensed the gravity of the situation, and all were aware of a national buckling on of armor.

Brother Kawabe had reached the age of sixty-six, but the thought of retirement never entered his mind. For more than forty years he had preached the gospel of

Christ, and he would continue to preach it as long as the Lord gave him breath. He was well aware of the political problems that harassed the nation and of the uncertain future it faced. He longed for revival, a sweeping movement of the Spirit, a Pentecost resulting in a great ingathering of souls. He longed to be free to evangelize. In the past, his evangelistic efforts — fruitful as they were — had been hampered by administrative responsibility, and he was beginning to tire.

He looked back across the decade of the 1920s, and marveled at what God had done. Five new churches had been established, Osaka First Church had burned and been rebuilt, the Osaka School for Evangelists had become the Japan Theological Seminary, and later a new plant was built at Maruyama-dori. There had been great revivals across the conference he supervised. One church, for example, pastored by Dr. Tsuchiyama, started with no members and in four years had grown to a membership of 130. It had been a tremendous decade of progress.

He looked ahead to the 1930s and sensed again the uncertainty that faced not only Japan but, perhaps, the whole world. And the burden for revival nearly crushed him. But Brother Kawabe was strong. He had never been sick for more than a day at a time in his whole life, and he determined then that his remaining years would be given wholly to evangelism.

He resigned the superintendency of the conference and, with it, every responsibility he could delegate to others. Mr. Tsuchiyama became the new superintendent.

Brother Kawabe had started with no members, no money, and little encouragement. In less than thirty years, he turned over to Mr. Tsuchiyama a strong and growing conference that reached into many areas of Japan. His philosophy of keeping the Osaka work under one church with outlying evangelistic halls probably held the work together in its early days and allowed him

59

guidance over the various units as they developed and grew.

By the time Tetsuji Tsuchiyama took the reins, these preaching points were strong Free Methodist societies, and he at once changed the pattern and gave them full church status. This also was probably an important step in the Japan work. Hence, there is little doubt as we study the record that God had his hand upon both men and was leading every step of the way.

Brother Kawabe was finally doing the work of an evangelist, unhampered and free. His schedule was exhausting, but his spirit and his strength seemed inexhaustible. He preached entire sanctification with neither fear nor favor, and the holiness movement in Japan grew steadily during the 1930s, reaching into many and varied Protestant communities.

The Great Depression of that decade, which affected every area of the world, paid its unwelcome visit to the islands of Japan. Brother Kawabe was quick to capitalize upon the devastating sense of insecurity it brought upon the people, many of whom had always reveled in their self-sufficiency. These people found no peace nor promise in their allegiance to the pagan gods they had always worshiped. Now they listened as Brother Kawabe and others presented the living Christ, loving and eternal, who had paid the supreme price for their redemption that they too might live forever.

The Kawabes made their way once more to Awaji Island where the Free Methodist Church in Japan had had its beginnings. Brother Kawabe recalled with a smile his first effort to evangelize on the island when it seemed an impossible task. How different it had become by 1930! The churches there were glowing and growing, and it was there, during those uncertain times, that Yosuke Matsuoka made many trips to visit his old friend and spiritual father, asking for counsel and prayer.

60

The stormy thirties passed quickly for the Kawabes, partly because they were busy, partly because they were growing old, but mostly because they were burdened for sweeping revival, and there was so little time left for them to labor in the Master's vineyard.

Then, too, the political climate was terrifying, and the future of the church loomed dark and altogether uncertain. By the mid-thirties, all Christian churches on the islands feared the dreadful days ahead in which anything could happen.

Church leaders sensed a need of huddling together to retain their identity, not as denominations, but as exponents of Christianity — ambassadors for Christ. In 1937 such an association of churches was established, adopting the name of *The United Church of Christ in Japan*. The Free Methodists quickly took advantage of this shelter but continued to evangelize in about the same pattern as before.

Then dawned the "flaming forties" with murky shadows hanging heavily over the tiny islands of the mighty empire. But the black, foreboding clouds, split by continuing streaks of lightning and rumbling with muffled peals of thunder, were not peculiar to Japan or even to the Orient. They dominated the atmosphere around the globe, shutting out for a while the warm sunlight of the ancient anthem: "On Earth Peace, Good Will to Men."

Winston Churchill voiced the sentiment of every national leader in the world when he bellowed, "I have nothing to offer but blood, toil, tears, and sweat," to a terrified British commonwealth. And again he said, "We shall fight on the beaches, we shall fight on the fields and in the streets; we shall never surrender."

And certainly these were the sentiments expressed by the mighty Tojo to the loyal people of Japan who had neither voice in the decisions nor answers to the problems that vexed their homeland.

How was a humble missionary preacher of the gospel of love, peace, and forgiveness to give counsel and advice to one of the most powerful, political figures of the hour, Yosuke Matsuoka? He did his best. Again and again, Brother Kawabe told his friend that he could pray only for God's will to be accomplished. And so it was that he was praying when zero hour of December 8 (December 7 on the other side of the International Date Line) exploded at Pearl Harbor in Hawaii, ushering in a four-year period of the most devastating holocaust in the history of the world.

The startling news of the surprise attack on the United States naval fleet lying peacefully at anchor that Sunday morning in 1941 was altogether confusing to the entire population, not only of Japan but of every nation. To Brother Kawabe it would have been an earthshaking revelation if he had not been so deeply rooted in the things of God. It seemed to him that his most earnest prayers had backfired, even as he was petitioning the throne of grace for peace on earth which, surely, he reasoned had to be the will of the Lord. A redeeming factor in his ability to hold steady in such an hour, however, was his abiding faith in a sovereign God who sees even the end from the beginning, whose ways are not man's ways, and whose ultimate purpose is unfolding with the dawn of every day.

He held steady, preaching as he had always preached, praying as he had always prayed, believing as he had always believed. At the end of the long night, he knew there would be a dawning.

American missionaries scurried home, of course, but they would return in time, and new ones would appear. A complete list of American missionaries who served the Free Methodist Church in Japan before the war is as follows:

1902 Rev. and Mrs. August Youngren
1903 Rev. and Mrs. W. F. Matthewson

1906 Rev. and Mrs. Sherman E. Cooper
1907 Miss Minnie K. Hessler
1908 Rev. and Mrs. Matthias Klein
1908 Rev. and Mrs. W. L. Meikle
1909 Miss Ruth Mylander
1911 Rev. and Mrs. R. W. Millikan
1917 Rev. and Mrs. Oliver R. Haslam
1918 Miss Lillian Pickens
1919 Rev. and Mrs. H. H. Wagner
1920 Miss Gertrude Aylard
1924 Rev. and Mrs. Frank Warren
1937 Miss Frances M. Hart

Following the war, the list included:
1948 Rev. and Mrs. Jacob DeShazer
1948 Miss Alice Fensome
1948 Rev. Oliver Haslam
1949 Dr. and Mrs. Elmer Parsons
1950 Miss Pearl Reid
1951 Miss Myrtle Anderson
1951 Rev. and Mrs. Harry Bullis
1952 Rev. and Mrs. Norman Overland
1952 Rev. and Mrs. Edward Skudler
1956 Dr. and Mrs. K. Lavern Snider

The War Years

Mitsuo Fuchida, a typical Japanese military man, fanatically devoted to his nation's cause and ready to live or die for his country, was chosen to lead the squadron of bombers in the Pearl Harbor attack. The scores of men under his command in the fleet of 183 aircraft were singled out for their bravery and devotion. Fuchida was said to be one of the world's best airmen, and the success of the deadly mission that awful morning clearly documented the assertion. Eighteen ships were sunk, 170 planes were destroyed, and 3,700 American servicemen lost their lives in the blazing inferno. All Japan heard the "good news" in blaring radio dispatches heralding the necessity and success of the awful invasion.

Brother Kawabe was heartsick. He knew that the attack had been no surprise to his friend Matsuoka, for whom he now prayed with greater fervency than ever. He prayed also for Mitsuo Fuchida, the man who led the attack and gave the orders.

He heard the daily reports of progress: America was on her knees. And this was only a beginning of a conquest, the reports continued, that would reach the far corners of the globe and make Japan the greatest nation the world had ever known.

But the enthusiastic prophecies were inaccurate. America soon got off her knees, although the war in the Pacific raged for months before she was in a position to retaliate.

Then came a day when another master airman was chosen to lead a squadron of bombers in the first U.S. raid over Japan. His name was James Doolittle, and the raiders he led were chosen for their bravery and devotion. The mission was successful, but a number of the men were forced to parachute to "safety" when fuel supplies ran out over China. They landed in Japanese-occupied territory and became prisoners of war. Some of these Americans died of natural causes; a few were executed. The rest remained in prison for forty months until the war finally ended. Among those prisoners of war was a young farmer from Oregon named Jacob DeShazer.

While DeShazer suffered in solitary confinement, air raids over Japan became common, resulting in massive destruction and death. Unfortunately, from the air, the Free Methodist school in Osaka resembled a factory, and on at least three occasions, it became the target of American bombardiers. Most able-bodied men in Japan were in uniform, and by the end of the war few of them were alive to return to their homes on the islands. A generation of men had been shot away in the brief span of less than four years from Pearl Harbor to Nagasaki.

It was during those many months of global warfare that the Doolittle bombardier, Jacob DeShazer, read and reread the pages of a borrowed Bible while languishing in solitary confinement. It was in that Japanese prison that "Jake" came to know the Christ of Calvary who suffered the most painful and disgraceful death devised by men in order that He might pay the price for man's redemption. It was there, weak, emaciated, and about to die a victim of malnutrition, loneliness, and fear, that DeShazer reached the place of repentance and accepted the free gift of salvation. Then it was that suddenly he realized he loved his enemies and longed for their redemption. And it was there that he vowed to return one day to Japan with Bibles, not with bombs; with the gospel, not with guns, to take the land with love.

After the war, Jake returned to America and enrolled in Seattle Pacific College to prepare for the ministry. Upon graduation, he was sent back to Japan as a missionary under the Free Methodist board. Later, DeShazer returned to America to complete seminary training at Asbury Seminary, Wilmore, Kentucky.

Eventually, the Free Methodist Church withdrew from the United Church of Christ in Japan to establish its identity as a denomination again. (See Appendix C.)

Tetsuji Tsuchiyama died in 1946, and another Free Methodist minister, Kaneo Oda, who had been evangelizing in China, returned to become the new conference superintendent. Later, when the Japanese church became a general conference, Kaneo Oda became its first bishop.

In the aftermath of the war, the revival that Brother Kawabe had long prayed for came with unprecedented force. It reached into every church as great crowds poured into the biggest auditoriums available or gathered in mammoth numbers for out-of-doors meetings.

Jacob DeShazer with his wife, Florence, spoke through interpreters to the multitudes. Their one intention was to spend their lives evangelizing in Japan, and as this paragraph is being written, more than thirty years after the close of the war, the DeShazers are still there, approaching retirement age but carrying on their soul-winning ministry.

The Kawabes were old but busy during the days of the postwar revival. We mentioned earlier that Brother Kawabe, while praying for his friend Matsuoka, prayed also for Captain Fuchida, the leader of the infamous attack on Pearl Harbor. The Lord let him live to see the answer to his prayer. About three years before Brother Kawabe slipped away to be with Jesus, Mitsuo Fuchida, an unhappy veteran who had been unable to find peace, was handed a tract which told the story of DeShazer's remarkable conversion in a Japanese prison camp. Fuchida was converted and spent the remainder of his life in a most effective evangelistic ministry. He died in 1976, thirty-five years after Pearl Harbor, twenty-six years after his conversion.

Brother Kawabe and his good companion were well aware that great revivals have always come and gone, and this one would wane and eventually nearly die in the pattern of every great awakening before it. Hence, while it remained and as long as their own strength lasted, they were determined to do their best.

Bokko Tsuchiyama, eldest son of Tetsuji Tsuchiyama, spent the war years in America where he received an excellent education. Following the war he returned home to experience a frustrating adjustment. Not only did his father's death bring sorrow into his life, but many of the young men of Japan who were near his age had died in battle. We can only imagine the loneliness that enveloped the young man's ambitious spirit. Helpful to him, though, was his marriage, which Brother Kawabe performed. Everything else was shattered. The school which Brother Kawabe had started and into which Bokko's father had poured his life was gone, a victim of bombings. Feeling a great urge to see his father's work and dream live again, Bokko gave himself wholeheartedly to assist in the reconstruction of the school, now called Osaka Christian College.

Young Tsuchiyama, like his father, was an excellent organizer. With order and precision he helped pick up the tangled threads, and soon the college lived again, a growing, glowing institution of higher learning. The Free Methodist Church of North America raised more than fifty thousand dollars to help rebuild the school. The Reverend E. C. John, field secretary of the General Missionary Board and later bishop, toured the North American churches to raise the money.

Bokko, however, faced a rough and lonely road. It was not easy, apparently, for him to work in harness with others, nor did he continue to embrace what to him seemed to be the narrow beliefs of his father's church. The eventual result was that he discontinued his relationship with the school and found employment elsewhere. It is impossible, of course, for us to sense the full frustrations of the times.

To help us at this point, we are fortunate to have a paper written in the 1940s by the Reverend Takuo Matsumoto of the International Council of Religious Education, Missionary Section. Mr. Matsumoto says:

Two thousand years of history in Japan has brought

about many changes, but there have been no changes as great as those since the defeat of Japan. The Japanese do not change easily, and this is a new experience to them. They realize they were naively disillusioned by the military force and now turn to the task of becoming a peace nation, a cultural nation, realizing the utter futility of war more than any other people, and feel that such a defeat was necessary to the life of the Japanese. Militarism is now completely wiped out; and out of Hiroshima, the city which suffered most bitterly from militarism, comes the plea and prayer for peace through the Peace Association. August 6, the day of the atom bombing of Hiroshima, is now commemorated as Peace Day. . . .

The sudden impoverishment that followed the defeat of Japan brought great confusion to all. The Japanese were never wealthy, but they were always self-supporting. Seventy cities were completely destroyed by bombs, and great inflation followed the closing of the armament factories where so many had been employed. The cost of living went so high the people were forced to sell their possessions to buy food, and their life became, as the Japanese express it, ''A life of peeling the skins of onions — you drop tears as you peel.'' War has been a destroyer of everything, and they are greatly discouraged and handicapped in their attempts to recover. It is still midnight in Japan, but they are looking for the dawn of a new day.

The state religion, of which the emperor was the center, went out with militarism, giving freedom of thought and worship to the people. Despite his denial of divinity the emperor is more popular than ever before. The form of government in Japan is to be much like that of England with the emperor retaining his position, but having little or no power. Both houses of the Diet, the House of Councillors and the House of Representatives, are elective, and of the 466 members the majority are from the National parties. Twenty is the voting age of both men and women, and since women have been granted the right to vote, thirty-nine women were elected to the Diet in the January, 1949, elections. The new Japan has an equal wage scale for men and women, and organized labor unions are legally recognized. Since freedom of speech has been granted, however, Communism has been growing and in the last election thirty-five communists were elected to the Diet.

In his report on his tour of Japan, Mr. Sherwood Eddy of the United States writes of an interview he had with Dr. Toyohiko Kagawa, who described the present situation in Japan as follows: "Japan today is undergoing an unparalleled, radical, social, and political revolution. Defeat has made us a new nation. When the emperor acknowledged defeat on August 15, 1945, the mythology of Japan was shattered. Japan's defeat would have brought on a bloody revolution were it not for the American occupation, but, had it not been for the defeat, the many reforms would not have been realized in less than one or two centuries. Although we are in the midst of an economical and political revolution, we have this, the glorious new constitution will in time be reduced to a mere scrap of paper. The next few years will be a period of crisis for the whole future in Japan."

This closing statement was strangely and profoundly prophetic.

Coronation

When the war ended, Brother Kawabe had reached the age of eighty-one, but nine excellent years were yet to be his before the Lord would call him home. He continued to preach. His advanced age, his tender spirit, his clear mental faculties, and his robust body gave power to his message and strength to his testimony. So, somewhat in the pattern of Oliver Wendell Holmes's *Wonderful One-Hoss Shay* — being equally strong in all his parts — he was to live on until old age would finally make its inevitable claim on him.

As most elderly people do, he found peace and pleasure in reminiscing. Bishop Elmer E. Parsons relates that Brother Kawabe loved to recall how it had been his custom during the early days in Fukura to go alone to a hilltop back of the village to pray and read the Word. On one occasion, feeling distressed because of the limited response of the people at Fukura, he came to the passage of scripture in Acts 18:9-10, ''Then spake the Lord to Paul in the night by a vision. Be not afraid, but speak, and hold not thy peace: for I am with thee, and no man shall set on thee to hurt thee: for I have much people in this city.'' He accepted this as God's promise to him for the town of Fukura and went back to his evangelism with renewed zeal and confidence.

In January 1949, missionary Oliver Haslam wrote the following:

Slip into the front seat of the pretty blue mission car and go with me for a ten-mile drive to the home of the venerable Brother and Sister Kawabe and watch their faces light up and their eyes sparkle, sometimes with tears of joy. Share with me in the warmth and fellowship of these two veterans of the cross, slowed down with the wear and tear of the years, yet always buoyant in spirit and with ever-broadening vision. To enter the Kawabe home is like entering the holy place; one cannot come out again without a touch of the glory which characterizes this godly couple.

The progress of the work in the early postwar period brought great joy to the heart of the aging Kawabe. He watched the reports with unusual interest, and one that particularly blessed his soul appeared in the July 1948 issue of the *Missionary Tidings*. Again, the writer is Oliver R. Haslam:

You will be interested to learn of the numerical progress of the work since the war. The first postwar year was very difficult and discouraging, but by the end of that year, with the return of Brother Oda from China and Brother Kaneda from Borneo, new courage began to be revived, and the work began to move, slowly at first and then with increasing acceleration. I called for an official report of the number of baptisms in each church during the calendar year of 1947. The total for all churches was 246. This is quite a remarkable figure in consideration of the fact that *all* of the churches were seriously affected by the war, and some of them were closed down entirely. The attendance at the big Nipponbashi Church in Osaka had dropped to a small fraction with a little group of faithful souls holding on in the midst of bitterness and tears and almost hopeless despair. Now it is flourishing again, although not up to the previous figure. There were 90 baptisms in this church in 1947. Truly the Lord of harvest is answering your prayers and honoring your gifts to Japan both in money and relief supplies.

You will be happily surprised to learn that up to May 1, 1948, the records show the receipt of 1,102 relief packages from the Free Methodist Church all over the United States and Canada. No other denomination comes even a close second to this, and the psychology of it is impressive here. Our workers are almost overwhelmed at your liberality and love. And as I tell here and there about the hundreds of letters from America which tell of earnest and constant prayers in their behalf, they are deeply grateful. It is true Japanese fashion to give gifts of appreciation for gifts received, and these dear people feel deeply their inability to show to the mother church in America their inexpressible sense of gratitude in some material way. But I have told them that all the churches in America want as an expression of their deep gratitude is that the entire church in Japan and all of its pastors and workers put everything they have into the task of gathering in the greatest possible harvest of souls while the doors are open wide and multitudes are openly receptive to the gospel. This they are doing in a remarkable measure. And we are expecting that during the year of 1948 the ingathering of souls will be phenomenal. Keep praying with us that this may be so. The signs are very encouraging, and the work is moving remarkably well.

Practically all of our pastors are very busy men. Some of them are getting along in years and cannot keep the pace of former years, but most of them are strong and energetic. Brother Kawabe at eighty-four years of age, though retired as a regular pastor, is still very much alive and very active. On the first Sunday of each month he preaches at the Osaka Second Church; on the third Sunday at the big

Nipponbashi Church where he was pastor for so many years, and on the other Sundays he goes here and there to other places where he is frequently called. He stands daily on the promise in Psalm 121:2, "My help cometh from the Lord, which made heaven and earth." Sister Kawabe takes for hers the twenty-third Psalm. They have started a mothers' meeting every Monday in their home. There were ten mothers at the first meeting. This number grew to fifty by the sixth meeting, held in January. Many people come to their home from miles around and even from distant places to visit and seek counsel. Sister Kawabe is a great helpmeet and a delightful entertainer. She is always giving away things that she has to people who seem more needy than she.

On the first of January the Lord gave to Brother Kawabe the promise of his community located on a hill called Senri Mountain. He read in Joshua 13:1, "Thou [Josuha] art old and stricken in years, and there remaineth yet very much land to be possessed." And then the words of Caleb in Joshua 14:12, "Now therefore give me this mountain, whereof the Lord spake in that day." So he felt that the Lord had promised him this mountain where he lives. During the month of January he was obliged to pay quite a heavy tax on his home. He did not have any money for this, and so committed the matter to the Lord, and by the time the tax was due he had more than enough. Thus the Lord continually supplies their needs, and I have seen to it that out of the relief supplies Brother and Sister Kawabe receive their share plus extra to use among the people of their community who are in need. They are always happy and rejoicing in the Lord. Brother Kawabe spends hours each day in prayer. His eyes are dimmed with age so that he can no longer read, but he constantly draws on the resources which he has stored up in his mind and heart across the years. . . .

Kawabe's last years were pleasant ones. Even though his sight yielded to the aging process, he was supremely happy as he reveled in the light of the gospel he had preached for nearly seventy years. He remained as active as his waning strength would permit.

Bishop Elmer E. Parsons, who was a missionary to Japan during the postwar period witnessed the "slowing down" process of the aging minister. He writes as follows:

> About two years before he passed away, Brother Kawabe had a great desire to preach again. He called on me and talked about it, so I volunteered to take him by car to the various churches to give him an opportunity to preach once more to the Free Methodist congregations. Week after week we visited the churches of the Osaka area, where I sat through a number of his sermons. Brother Kawabe would stand behind the pulpit with a Bible in front of him even though he couldn't see a word on the page. Then he would begin his message with a good strong voice and with marked attention from the people. He would preach for at least an hour and refer to the passages of Scripture by giving chapter and verse, allowing the people to check as he would call upon his great memory for the portions of God's Word which he loved. This was an excellent experience for our people, and it tied them to the past in a wonderful way.
>
> Since it had been a number of years since he visited many of these churches, this was like a coronation series of messages.

About a year before his death, Brother Kawabe attended the dedicatory service of a new auditorium at the

Osaka Christian College. He was asked to speak. He sat in a chair facing the audience and, among other things, stated firmly a desire to preach the gospel until he toppled over. His voice was strong and resonant, and it was said that he used a very dramatic Japanese word for this last expression. The moment was as unforgettable as the words were prophetic.

Actually, he never toppled over. He simply ran down like an old clock. During his last days he slept except for brief periods of consciousness. On one such occasion, he raised up suddenly on his elbow and began to preach. It was apparent that he was unaware of anything or anyone around him as his voice rang out in a message directed to little children. When he finished the touching sermon, he slept again, but not for long. Upon awakening, he raised up and preached again; this time an evangelistic message to sinners, which he closed with an invitation to come to Jesus. It seemed to those around him that he had used the last of his waning strength as once again he drifted into peaceful repose, but it wasn't so. There was yet another sermon to deliver, a message to the saints. This final discourse was brief but no less positive than the others as he exhorted the people to put God first in every area of their lives. All three messages were typical of the man, embodying the three great themes of his lifelong ministry.

Then Brother Kawabe slept again to awaken within the portals of heaven, to rise up this time in the glorious presence of the Christ he had served so faithfully and long.

Mitsu Kawabe wrote that his father was transferred to his heavenly reward at 11:28 P.M. January 27, 1953, at the age of ninety.

"He really fought a good fight," the son stated proudly. "He finished the course and kept the faith. He deserves a crown of righteousness."

APPENDIX A
Understanding Japan
by
K. Lavern Snider

Who can understand Japan? To understand and describe a nation in terms of geographical features and economic progress is relatively an easy task. But a nation in essence is its people with their history, their culture, their sense of identity, responsibility, and destiny.

Ever since the doors of Japan were thrown open to the outside world in 1853 with the forced entrance of the United States of America's Commodore Perry, the world has diligently tried to understand Japan. Businessmen, politicians, and educators have applied themselves to the task of understanding and interpreting Japan to the rest of the world. Written at a time when the world desperately needed to understand Japan — during World War II — *The Chrysanthemum and the Sword* has become a classic.[1] Indeed, some Japanese themselves, especially in the post World War II years, have vigorously set themselves to understanding and interpreting Japan to the world.[2] I too, during sixteen years of missionary service in Japan have learned much about Japan and have much more to learn.

Through the following paragraphs I want to open the windows of the readers' understanding, at least a little, to the people of this great nation.

I. Enigmatic Japan

The international image of Japan still seems to be strangely blurred. Tourists to Japan are shocked when they are introduced to Japan's world of concrete, earthquake-proof, high-rise apartments and office buildings, when they ride in the world's fastest train (the name of the train is "Light"), and when they attend cultural performances of unexcelled quality. Vast cities hum busily under a pall of smog, producing huge quantities of sophisticated goods in sprawling, efficient factories, while minutes away by train farmers still plant rice seedlings by hand to feed the nation. Ancient koto and shamisen vie with the guitar for the listening ear of the Japanese public. The typical new home in the suburbs blends ancient and modern architectural design. One finds it difficult to know which to call the national sport: sumo wrestling, baseball, or bowling.

Japan is a nation in a hurry as evidenced by impatient commuters who push to enter subway cars before the doors close, for they cannot wait until the next train which comes but one minute later. However, millions of Japanese still find time for leisurely cultivation of traditional arts, medieval military skills, the ancient tea ceremony, and even Zen meditation.

The missionary and businessman from abroad soon learn that there are unique elements in the culture of the nation, ancient and not about to be surrendered. Neither in image nor in reality has classical Japan been obliterated during the 120-year process of merging into a dynamic and modern nation commanding the respect of the entire world. Enigmatic Japan!

To many Japanese themselves, Japan is enigmatic. This is especially true of post World War II youth as evidenced, for example, by the many factions among student self-governing organizations arising out of divergent understanding and ideals for society. Lofty idealism of college years, however, quickly melts away when the student, following graduation casts his lot with the giant corporation, accedes to company policy, and begins his climb to success and the good life.

Centuries have produced rigid patterns of politeness and respect for age and position. Students stand to their feet when the teacher appears at the classroom door; the school graduation ceremony is precisely defined and incorporates elements which have been refined over many years. However, a group of radical students having cast aside respect for their elders and superiors, occasionally have taken captive a school administrator to extract from him confessions of guilt and promises of reform in accordance with their demands. A prestigious college graduation may suddenly be interrupted by the same radicals who care little or nothing for generally accepted graduation formalities.

Probably the enigma of Japan is no more evident than in the constant struggle between collectivism and individualism. Human relations are enormously important in Japanese society. All of life is under constant mental restraint and preoccupation with one's friends and neighbors; and human relations, at least in the eyes of the outsider, become very cumbersome. Expressed disagreement with a superior is a rarity; "Everyone has agreed" is the common way of recording a decision in a business meeting. Consensus is the norm. However, one can readily see that this common procedure can create a real procedural problem when a matter of major import is under consideration. Opposition parties in the national government have resolved the problem on occasion by entire party absenteeism until the government-sponsored bill has been passed.

Japanese collectivism has its roots in feudalism, the nation at one time having had 250 principalities, each with its own feudal lord, retainees, and serfs and all members of each domain pledged to cohesion, loyalty, and commitment. In the last quarter of a century the nation has fast become individualistic in the individual's search for personal identity and pursuit of greater material well-being. Naturally this trend for individualism is still crude and unpolished. Both parents and children can testify to the tension which arises in the choosing of a marriage partner. Parents may feel acutely their sense of responsibility in choosing the partner; the son or daughter may claim that this choice is solely his to make. Again, one may wonder about the various elements that entered into the decision of a youth to commit suicide. Was the element of individual assertion in this one final act a dominant element? Or was the dominant element a confession by this act of the youth's inability to conform sufficiently to the collective will?

When it comes to international relationships, the enigmatic problem looms large. Japan does not consider mainland China the threat that the United States of America does. Rather, she respects China's growing power and prestige, this factor added to her ancient debt of gratitude to China for her cultural heritage through the centuries.

Enigmatic Japan! To the foreigner and to the Japanese themselves this is true. But Japan has always been an enigma. And so has every other nation. This fact, however, serves as a stimulus for striving to better understand other nations and other people.

II. **Reverence for History**

Occidentals look to the future; Orientals look to the past, for they have a keen sense of being "debtors to the ages."[3] Until the Japanese emperor disavowed his divinity at the close of World War II, emperors had been worshiped as divine from 600 B.C. when Jimmu Tenno, leader of the powerful Yamamoto clan, established himself as the sole ruler of central Japan. According to the ancient records and traditions of the Japanese, the emperor is a descendant in unbroken line from the sun goddess, Amaterasu Omikami, and the islands of Japan have a divine origin, as have also the Japanese people. Lingering elements of the divine concept are to be found in the religious beliefs and daily living of the Japanese.

Tenrikyo, one of the new religious sects with roots in Shrine Shintoism, identifies the spot with religious symbols where the earth was supposedly created. To this sacred place located at Tenri city, headquarters of the sect, multitudes converge twice monthly from all parts of Japan to worship mother creator, symbolized by the sun. Nihonism, which perceives the Japanese people as distinct from all others, suggests also that deeply engrained in Japanese psychology is a strong link with Japan's past. The book, *The Japanese and the Jew,* gives considerable attention to this subject of Nihonism.[4]

The Japanese feel and live in constant communion with the past. There is an intimate bond between the people of today and their ancestors, a feeling for the constant presence of the past and bonds with the ancestors. Ancestor worship, seen in this light, may not be wholly directed toward ancestors; instead, it is a "ritual avowal of man's great indebtedness to all that has gone before."[5] Foreign tourists often become weary of being shown temple after temple and shrine after shrine because for them history does not command the respect that it does for the Japanese. The multitudes of Japanese tourists who frequent the same temples and shrines come to worship but, more significantly, come to pay their respect to all who have contributed to the nation. Yasukuni Shrine, where fallen Japanese soldiers from wars of the past one hundred years are enshrined, is drawing an increasing number of visitors. The very fact that the visitor comes to pay his respect to the fallen in battle, though he may not know whether any of his own ancestors are among the fallen, indicates his reverence for history and his debt to previous generations.

Debts to ancestors of many centuries, to the feudal lords of history — in short, to the rich historical past — these are always owing. The Japanese from early childhood is taught that he must dedicate his life to the repayment of a debt of such great magnitude that he knows he can never discharge it. Thus there is an inescapability from the obligations and the constant pressure to conform to the traditions of the past which have been inherited at such great cost.

III. Sense of Patriotism

Closely akin to the Japanese reverence for history is the sense of patriotism. This sense of patriotism was not a hasty development in the years preceding World War II, necessary for gaining support of the people for military conquests. Rather, the sense of patriotism which has characterized the Japanese people through their long history was made concrete and utilized to attain national and military goals in World War II. This patriotism has been called by the Japanese themselves the ''genius'' or the ''spirit of Japan.''[6] The spirit and prowess of the early conquerors and particularly of Jamamoto, the dominant clan from which the first emperor emerged, have left an indelible impression upon the people.

Historically, the Japanese sense of patriotism has included ''the Japanese race divinely endowed, a superior culture, a superior racial stock, an unbroken continuity, and a beneficent destiny guaranteed under the aspect of eternity.''[7] Before and during World War II, patriotism came to be virtually the faith of the Japanese nation. Christians who claimed they owed a greater loyalty to Jesus Christ suffered intensely for their faith. For a Christian educator reflecting on his own feelings during those most difficult years, ''The Christian torn between two loyalties and entirely cut off from overseas contacts, was in many ways an 'unwilling patriot' — a dangerous position to occupy.''[8] Shrine worship and Japanese patriotism increasingly became a unity, and if one should choose not to appear at the state shrine and participate in the shrine ceremony, he was marked as unpatriotic and dangerous to the family life. The spirit which enabled Japan's armies to bring vast territories into subjection and which later, when the tide of battle was against her, enabled her to fight to the bitter end was the dynamic of Japanese patriotism.

Loyalty and a sense of patriotism are deeply engrained in the personality of every Japanese. The Japanese citizen is consciously or unconsciously bound to others and subject to powerful patriotic influences. He is controlled by his superiors because he owes them loyalty, by his equals because he is a member of the group to which he belongs, and to his inferiors because he must necessarily respect public opinion. He may occasionally struggle to free himself from these fetters, but he never is completely free to choose and to act. Conformity prevents embarrassment, and this being the case, the usual Japanese is shrewd in estimating all the factors involved in the situation and will do nothing that will give rise to the charge of disloyalty, arouse criticism, lessen his chances of success, or in essence, to indicate that he is disloyal to his particular sector of the society.

Group values and innate sense of loyalty constitute a unity. Japanese culture stresses group values in contrast to the Westerner's individualism, since group solidarity, loyalty to the society, has long been considered in Japan as taking precedence over individual interest. This is evidenced by the child submitting to the family wish; the family as a part of the village must be true to the interests of the village; and in matters of national concern, the duty of all subjects is to support the nation. The promotion of this loyalty system is perpetrated today, for example, by the business company when employees assemble before they begin the day's work to engage together in calisthenics, to sing heartily the company's song, and to repeat in unison company slogans.

IV. Religious Devotion

The three major religions of Japan are Shintoism, Buddhism, and Christianity. Christianity was a relative latecomer and accounts at the present time for 1 million believers in a total population of 107 million.

In Japan, from the beginning of recorded history, the mysterious dynamism of the universe is called *kami,* that element of power which inhabits and activates all unusual objects and persons. In Shintoism, Japan's indigenous religion, this primitive animism has been called "the way of the gods." The *kami* reside in village shrines and inhabit peculiarly shaped trees and rocks and every waterfall; they make special appearances on special festival occasions. Shintoism at its peak venerated the sun goddess and demanded worship of the emperor, who was considered a direct descendant of the sun goddess. Men who have earned the gratitude of a significant number of Japanese have been deified and thus considered objects of worship including rulers, warriors, inventors, and other great benefactors.

Shintoism originally carried little or no philosophical content, nor did it teach an ethical code. It was engaged in purely for the practical results it yielded. By the manipulation of the gods, one was assured of protection and sustenance for maintaining life. With the passing of the centuries, Shintoism has undergone considerable change, but traces of animism are still to be seen — in the preservation of a sacred tree in the middle of a busy thoroughfare with traffic lanes diverted around the tree or in a Japanese *haiku* (distinctive Japanese poetic form), where man is identified with a crow, a frog, or even a withering willow. On the popular level, Shintoism features prominently in the lives of the people at important stages of life such as when the child turns three, five, or seven, when the youth comes of age at twenty years, and at the time of marriage.

Buddhism, Japan's second major religion, came from China by way of Korea in the sixth century. Pure Buddhism is hard to find in Japan today, because through the centuries Shintoism and imported Buddhism have melted together. The traditional eclectic-syncretic bent of the Japanese mind makes it relatively easy for a person to be Shintoist and Buddhist at the same time, a fact which creates a problem for the national census taker in respect to religious identification.

Through Buddhism Japan also received from China a cultural inheritance including architecture, painting, bronze casting, wood carving, tapestry, and silk culture.

Funeral rites are invariably conducted by a Buddhist priest. Buddhism is said to be the religion for death; in contrast, Shintoism is the religion for persons while they are living.

Although Confucianism, strictly speaking, is not a religion, its ethical teachings and evolved religious meanings have been added to the religious life of Japan as a further inheritance from China. The teachings of Confucius have given strength to the Japanese family system and have helped to place ancestors in a firm position of reverence. And too, Confucianism, with its emphasis on the drive for success and the importance of personal discipline based on work and formal education to achieve success, clearly indicates a subtle religious significance for the Japanese.

The new religions of Japan, having their roots in Shintoism and Buddhism and numbering in the hundreds, are predominantly postwar phenomena, having made a bold appeal to the masses with phenomenal success. The new religions are indigenous and deeply rooted in Japanese psychology; at the same time they are eclectic, unhesitatingly adapting and absorbing the religious teachings of other groups including Christianity. Each sect has a historical founder, it own sacred writings, generally written or voiced by the founder but many times added to or interpreted by later leaders. Each sect claims it is the only true religion and thus quite distinct from all others. Predominantly the new religions are utilitarian, performing rituals at important events such as birth, marriage, and death; they promise devotees health, wealth, and happiness.

Christianity was first introduced to Japan by Frances Xavier in 1549. So great was the appeal of Christianity upon its entrance to Japan that by the middle of the seventeenth century there were 750 thousand believers including a large number of rulers and the upper classes of society. However, before many decades of Christian history in Japan had passed, Christians came to be looked upon as suspect, a danger to the best interests of the country, as spies for foreign powers. Persecution set in. As persecution intensified, the doors of Japan were closed, not only to Christianity, the foreigner's religion, but to all but a few foreigners. Only the port of Nagasaki was to remain open to the occasional Dutch and Chinese shipping vessels for a period of two hundred years.

In spite of the martyrdom of tens of thousands of Christians before and during the closed-door period, Christianity went underground. And when at last, after two hundred years of silence, Christianity could emerge again, there was considerable reason to believe that Christianity had not been obliterated as the rulers had intended.

Protestant Christianity followed on the heels of Admiral Perry's forced entrance into Japan in 1858. Since this date there has not been the phenomenal growth of the Christian church, neither Roman Catholic nor Protestant, as was the case when the gospel first entered Japan. Nevertheless, there was a steady growth under the leadership of both missionaries and nationals until the years preceding and during World War II when the

Christian church suffered a considerable setback under the military government.

Christian believers of all faiths suffered intensely during the war years, as individuals and together, for their faith. Many pastors were imprisoned; some died of malnutrition during their imprisonment. With the defeat of Japan and subsequent reforms, everything associated with the old regime including Japan's traditional religions came to be discredited as having failed to give victory to the nation. In the religious vacuum thus created, people were ready to listen to the message of Christianity because they were really heart hungry for the gospel or because they posited military success as issuing from religious belief. People flocked to Christian meetings both large and small, and many professed conversion. Increases in church membership were experienced by prewar denominations. New missions entered Japan, and new denominations were created. In more recent years there has been a leveling off of church growth for whatever the reasons. Church membership is more than 1 million, the Roman Catholic Church accounting for one-third of the number, and the Protestant churches, the other two-thirds.

During the past 114 years of Christianity in Japan the influence of the Christian church has been exceedingly disproportionate to its recorded membership. Although church membership records show the nation to be 1 percent Christian, government reports show a 3 percent Christian church affiliation. Many prestigious educational institutions were founded by the Christian church. Several Christian hospitals were founded and operate under Christian auspices; many social reforms were championed by Christian leaders, and the moral principles of the nation have been strangely influenced by Christianity. Presently twenty members of the lower house in the Japanese Diet are Christians.

A century and two decades ago, who would have dreamed of there being a Christian church in that hermit nation? But the church is there today, a community of professing Christians of more than a million believers. Surrounding the church is a much larger circle including several millions of people whose lives have been affected, some superficially, others deeply, by the message of the gospel. The soil of this nation has been prepared through several generations of Christian witness and activity and which in faith I sincerely believe will bear an abundant harvest in the closing decades of this century.

FOOTNOTES

1. Ruth Benedict, *The Chrysanthemum and the Sword* (Boston: Houghton Mifflin Co., 1946), p. 324.
2. Takaaki Aikawa and Lynn Leavenworth, *The Mind of Japan* (Valley Forge: Judson Press, 1967), 159 pp.; and Ichiro Kawasaki, *Japan Unmasked* (Tokyo: Charles E. Tuttle Co., 1969), 231 pp.
3. Ruth Benedict, *The Chrysanthemum and the Sword* (Boston: Houghton Mifflin Co., 1946).
4. Isaiah Benda-Dasan, *The Japanese and the Jew* (New York: Weatherhill, 1972). Translated into English by Richard L. Gage.
5. Ibid., p. 98.
6. G. H. Moule, *The Spirit of Japan* (London: Student Volunteer Missionary Union, 1913), p. 17.
7. N. Kishimoto, "The Future of Religions in Japan," from W. W. Griffis, *Religions in Japan* (New York: Scribners), p. 97.
8. Aikawa and Leavenworth, *The Mind of Japan,* ix.

APPENDIX B
Religions of Japan
by
Ruth Mylander

The Japanese are a very religious people, and symbols of worship are to be found everywhere. The principal religions are Shintoism and Buddhism. Shintoism, meaning "the way of the gods," is the primitive or original religion of Japan. It has no moral teaching except patriotism and veneration of the ancestors. It has no theory as to a future state of rewards and punishments and makes no appeal to reason or emotion.

The chief objects of worship are the sun-goddess, Amaterasu, and the Amaterasu emperor as her descendant. Spirits of the dead are believed to have power to bring sorrow or joy to the living and are therefore worshiped or propitiated. As Shinto is linked with the land and love of beauty, so every tree, mountain, and river has its own god.

There are no images, but there is an emblem of deity in a mirror, sword, and jewel, kept out of sight of the public, in the inner part of the national shrine at Ise, in a chest not unlike the ark. These are said to be insignia handed by the sun-goddess to the first emperor. Shinto shrines are very simple, made of white wood, with thatched roofs and no ornamentation. There is one arch or more called *torii,* at the entrance. According to one authority, the number of shrines was 190,803.

Before each shrine there is a bowl of holy water into which the worshiper dips his fingers as a symbol of purification. Shinto teaches the native purity of the Japanese heart and that to follow one's own instincts and be loyal to the emperor is all that is necessary for salvation.

Since Shinto had already been made a cult of national

loyalty, it was easy for the warlords to use it in the planning of the late war. A state Shinto with government-paid priests was instituted, and the bow required of all loyal citizens was declared not to be religious but only to be an act of patriotism. After surrender and occupation, a directive to the Japanese cabinet declared, "All national funds for the support of Shinto and state religion are to be withdrawn." So state Shinto is no more, and at the present, according to late reports, the shrine and grounds at Ise are divided into living quarters. The big shrine at Tokyo is deserted, and the priests are said to be having a hard time making a living.

Buddhism, "the way of Buddha," had its birth in India, and came to Japan A.D. 552 by way of China and Korea. Finding Shinto well established, it got its hold by identifying the Shinto deities with Buddhist saints and demigods. In Japan as elsewhere, Buddhism had the peculiar genius of adapting itself to existing conditions. It is called the religion of the common man.

Its theology is complex; its teaching of rewards and punishments seems to be that after death a person is born again into something higher or lower, according to how he has lived; it may be a person, an animal, or an insect. The highest attainment is the extinction of all desire, and after an endless cycle of transmigrations, the ultimate goal is to be absorbed into "Nirvana" or nonentity.

In contrast to the simple Shinto shrine is the elaborate heaviness of the Buddhist temple. Its entrance is marked by a ponderous red gate, flanked by two hideous guardian deities. The temples are large with massive tiled roofs and corridors of gleaming polished wood. According to Galen M. Fisher, "Like the cathedrals of Europe the most exquisite architectural creations in Japan were the temples erected for Buddhist worship . . . with some artists lavishing their lives upon them." Kyoto, a city of temples has many that are costly and beautiful: one has 33,333 images of Buddha; a thousand of them are five feet high with other smaller ones placed on arms, in ears, and so forth. But the most beautiful and gorgeous temples are in Nikko. At one time there were more than 71 thousand temples, with 54 thousand priests.

Images of Buddha are the chief objects of worship; some are of huge proportions. The largest, fifty feet high, is in Kamakura. Worship consists mostly of bowing, standing or kneeling, clapping hands, burning incense, offering coins, and ringing bells. Some of the more earnest worshipers may give an offering to the priest and remain kneeling a long time while the priest mumbles prayers and strikes gongs. But we never see any joy or satisfaction on the face of the worshiper.

Buddhists have borrowed much from Christianity, such as preaching services, Sunday schools, YMCA, and Christian hymns with little change, such as "Buddha Loves Me." Buddhism is divided into twelve chief sects and many minor ones. One sect teaches that the goal of endeavor is not nonentity but is like a Western paradise, a land of joy and pure delight obtained by simple faith in Amida. The devotee needs only to repeat over and over the magic name of Amida. Another sect lays strong emphases on good works; still another stresses healing, like Christian Scientists. The end of the war found Buddhism bankrupt and with no power or plan to reconstruct Japan. Shintoism and Buddhism are not as separate and distinct as the above might indicate; often quite a mixture of practices and forms of worship are to be found in the same temple or shrine, and a great many belong to both religions.

Confucianism, "the way of the sage," came from China in the fifth century. It is a religion of the educated, if it can be called a religion (it has no god and deals only with morals). Confucius, a very great teacher, taught practical virtues, such as patriotism, obedience, filial piety, and loyalty on the part of the ordinary man, and benevolence and justice on the part of rulers. Confucianism played a great part in the thinking of the educated man, and these cardinal virtues were taught in the schools; so they greatly influenced youth.

Many other religions and cults, with large numbers of adherents, sprang up before the war, and since the war there are said to be many more strange cults mixed with Christianity, superstition, and ridiculous practices.

APPENDIX C

Free Methodism and the United Church of Japan

by
Byron S. Lamson

At its 1952 annual session, the conference of the Japan Free Methodist Church voted to withdraw from the Kyodan, the United Church of Japan. This is the story behind that historic action.

The Japanese government proclaimed its "Religious Bodies' Law" on April 1, 1940. This law provided the following: (1) Each religious sect or denomination must have one national head; (2) There may not be less than 5,000 members in fifty churches in each recognized denomination. Following the passage of this law, Protestant leaders in Japan began studying this whole problem, and on June 24 and 25, 1941, in the Presbyterian Church in Tokyo they proceeded to organize the Church of Christ in Japan (Nippon Kirisuto Kyodan). More than thirty denominations participated in this joint action.

The Church of Christ in Japan was a child of wartime necessity, created at this time by the church leaders themselves to protect the smaller denominations and to create a strong, united Protestant voice. There were eleven divisions in the Kyodan, each composed of theologically like-minded denominations. During the war the denominational groupings were abolished, and an overall church organization was substituted. The Free Methodist Church in Japan was a part of this organization.

In 1946 General Douglas MacArthur revoked the "Religious Bodies' Law." Immediately following this, there were several withdrawals from the Kyodan, among them The Salvation Army, Lutherans, Nazarenes, Southern Baptists, and Presbyterians. However, in 1950 approximately 60 percent of the Protestant church membership in Japan were identified with the Kyodan. But all was not peaceful.

Division of Forces

Within the Kyodan two forces struggled for expression. One group desired the Kyodan to develop as a strong national church, whereas the other group desired the Kyodan to become a loosely organized federation of independent and self-supporting churches. However, at the general assembly in October 1950, the federation turned down the plea for a loose federation on the ground that this would result in ultimate disunity. There was much dissatisfaction with this decision.

In March 1951, twenty Presbyterian churches withdrew from the Kyodan on the ground that denominations were not recognized in the general assembly and that the Kyodan lacked an adequate creed. It was felt also that there was too much foreign influence in the Kyodan itself and that self-support of churches was being weakened by too strong an over-church organization. It was apparent that leaders in the Kyodan were striving for a powerful, strong, central church organization which is more than was originally planned in the Kyodan legislation.

The Free Methodist Church in Japan did not choose to withdraw from the Kyodan immediately following the war. They had received many benefits from the cooperative relationship during the war and after. Many felt that their influence in the United Church of Japan was greater than it would be if they should withdraw. It was also felt that the Kyodan would become a federation and that as such the Free Methodist Church should be happy to have this larger fellowship in presenting a united front on social and religious matters in Japan.

Birth of Free Methodist Kai

After the war the Free Methodist Missionary Board contributed liberally to the rebuilding of churches, to the support of pastors, and to the reconstruction of church and college buildings which had been destroyed.

After 1945 several preliminary steps were taken to insure the perpetuation of Free Methodist ideals in the Japan church. A corporation was established whereby Free Methodist workers held title to Free Methodist Church property. Also, a Free Methodist Kai or Conference was organized within the Kyodan and approved by the Kyodan. In 1950 the constitution of the Japan Free Methodist Church was revised in harmony with the Free Methodist *Book of Discipline.*

Contrary to the anticipation of the Japan Conference, the Kyodan moved in the direction of a strong centralized church rather than that of a federation. At the 1951 conference of the Free Methodist Kai it was decided to make one more effort to encourage the Kyodan to decentralize. A petition was presented, and a committee was appointed to confer with leaders of the United Church. This was done on April 25, 1952. The Kyodan leaders advised the Free Methodist committee that it was very unlikely that such action would be taken by the Kyodan at its October 1952 meeting.

Position of Missionary Board

Before the convening of the 1952 annual conference, the presiding officer, Missionary Secretary Byron S. Lamson, was requested to meet with the Board of Administration, with the pastors, and with a representative group of laymen to discuss the entire matter. The position of the Missionary Board was that this was a problem for the Japan Free Methodist Church. The church in Japan had nearly sixty years of history. There were strong leaders in the church who understood the Japan situation and also knew the doctrines and practices of the Free Methodist Church. Some of them had been educated in America, and others had visited this country.

Christianity is a small force in Japan, and it is necessary for Christian movements to present a united voice on reform matters, world peace, and social legislation. At the same time the Free Methodists in Japan did not want to surrender their theology, the appointment of their pastors, and the ordination of their ministers to those who were not sympathetic either in theology or in practical Christian living.

Conference Action

The Japanese leaders discussed the problem from every angle. Many of the committee meetings ran into the small hours of the morning. It seemed clear to all, finally, that withdrawal from the Kyodan was necessary since the Kyodan was in effect a church. There was some difference of opinion regarding the time to announce the withdrawal and the exact method to pursue. The decision finally came when the Board of Administration brought to the conference a recommendation. The Board of Administration recommended as follows:

Article I. We recommend the establishment of a Religious Corporation to be known as the Japan Free Methodist Church, according to the Revised Constitution of the Japan Free Methodist Church as adopted in 1951.

The churches of the Free Methodist Conference that are not members of the Kyodan must establish the Japan Free Methodist Church and ask approval of the conference for a Religious Corporation. The need is urgent. Therefore, we recommend the establishment and incorporation of the Japan Free Methodist Church.

Article II. We recommend that the Free Methodist

churches belonging to the Kyodan withdraw from the same and join the Japan Free Methodist Church which is to be incorporated.

After these recommendations the Board of Administration appended an argument for the recommendation which reads in part:

In order to maintain a united witness regarding Communism, the Roman Church, and moral and social reform, it is proper for us to be associated with other Protestant churches for cooperative action. However, it is difficult to be associated with other churches whose theology, standards of conduct for church members, and methods of evangelism are out of harmony with our traditions. Ultimately we would be influenced by this association.

Since the Free Methodist Church is extended around the world, we would like to be associated with other churches which are Free Methodist. We negotiated with the Kyodan as requested by the conference last year. We petitioned the Kyodan to reorganize as an association of churches. Whether this proposition is approved or rejected, we need in either case a Religious Corporation. Local churches are now required by law to incorporate. We need the incorporation of the Japan Free Methodist Church.

In conclusion we recommend withdrawal from the Kyodan. We also recommend every church of the conference to join the Japan Free Methodist Church. We will cooperate with other spiritual and evangelical churches of Christ for more effective work.

The conference discussed the recommendation from many angles. When the vote was taken it was a very strong one. The few dissenting were in the main the ones who favored withdrawal from the Kyodan, but at a later date. The Japan Conference made the decision. . . .

–from the Missionary Tidings, September, 1952